Parenting Issues

ISSUES

Volume 124

Series Editor

Craig Donnellan

Assistant Editor

Lisa Firth

Independence

Educational Publishers
Cambridge

First published by Independence
PO Box 295
Cambridge CB1 3XP
England

British Library Cataloguing in Publication Data
Parenting Issues – (Issues Series)
I. Donnellan, Craig II. Series
306.8'74

ISBN 1 86168 363 4

Printed in Great Britain
MWL Print Group Ltd

Layout by
Lisa Firth

Cover
The illustration on the front cover is by
Don Hatcher.

CONTENTS

Introduction

Parenting Issues is the one hundred and twenty fourth volume in the **Issues** series. The aim of this series is to offer up-to-date information about important issues in our world.

Parenting Issues looks at some of the most relevant issues and problems with modern parenting, as well as the changing structure of the family in the UK today.

The information comes from a wide variety of sources and includes:
Government reports and statistics
Newspaper reports and features
Magazine articles and surveys
Website material
Literature from lobby groups
and charitable organisations.

It is hoped that, as you read about the many aspects of the issues explored in this book, you will critically evaluate the information presented. It is important that you decide whether you are being presented with facts or opinions. Does the writer give a biased or an unbiased report? If an opinion is being expressed, do you agree with the writer?

Parenting Issues offers a useful starting-point for those who need convenient access to information about the many issues involved. However, it is only a starting-point. Following each article is a URL to the relevant organisation's website, which you may wish to visit for further information.

*****

Bringing up children

Bringing up children is more difficult now than it was a generation ago

- *Saga research reveals that almost three-quarters of baby boomers say it was easier to raise a family in their day*
- *37% of today's parents feel guilty about having to work*
- *A quarter of parents don't think their children get enough attention from them*

A new study from *SAGA Magazine* reveals that an overwhelming number of today's parents[1] and grandparents believe it is more difficult to raise a family now than it was a generation ago. Over two-thirds (68%) of today's parents say it was easier to bring up children in their parents' day and nearly three-quarters (73%) of grandparents agree with them.

The reasons for this consensus are mixed, with the biggest cause thought to be that children today are more materialistic and have higher expectations (81%), closely followed by the increased cost of living (80%). Other explanations include the possibility that we generally have busier lives (73%) and increasingly dispersed families; the close family support network is not so easy to call upon (29%).

Working parents

One of the reasons that families appear much busier now is the increased reliance on two incomes meaning that both parents have to work. More than a quarter of respondents[2] (28%) say both parents work full time and one-third (33%) of households have one full-time and one part-time worker. When asked what effect this has on their families, an overwhelming majority (82%) said they thought their children were happy, but 37% confessed that it affected them (i.e. the parents), as they tended to feel constantly guilty. Nearly a quarter (24%) believed that

14% felt they were not always there when their children needed them

their children did not get enough attention from them and 14% felt that they were not always there when their children needed them most.

Comparing this with the childhood of today's parents, nearly one-third (32%) had one parent who stayed at home full-time and a further two-fifths (39%) had one part-time and one full-time working parent. They are, however, interestingly divided about how much difference a parent in the home makes. Almost half (46%) said it was beneficial, and (41%) said it would have made no difference either way.

Over four-fifths (86%) of today's parents thought their parents spent enough time with them when they were children.

Today's grandparents

A great number of today's parents (93%) said their parents make good grandparents; with a quarter qualifying this by stating that they spend a lot of time with their grandchildren. Despite the fact that families are more spread out than ever before, grandparents are clearly still providing an essential support role for their children, with 14% of parents saying their parents are always there when they are needed to help with the care of grandchildren.

Andrew Goodsell, Chief Executive of SAGA commented: 'It's easy to say that today's parents are of the "have it all generation", that in many cases parents combine good careers with having a family. The reality is that many find it hard to juggle every aspect of their busy lives without some help. Our study shows that, despite the changes in family life over the years, grandparents continue to fulfill a vital support role in the family.'

Notes

1. Current parents are those aged between 16 and 49, with parents aged 50 to 65 and children aged 15 or less.
2. Both parents or a single parent.

3 November 2005

- Information from SAGA. For more information see www.saga.co.uk.

© *SAGA*

'BYE DARLING, BE A GOOD BOY!'

Today's parents less strict than a generation ago

Information from SAGA

- **91% of grandparents think their children make good parents;**
- **But 45% of grandparents would choose different parenting tactics.**

A new study of parenting skills from SAGA has revealed that while most grandparents believe their children are doing a good job of raising their grandchildren, almost half (45%) of grandparents said they would like to change something about the way that their grandchildren are being brought up.

Even though most grandparents rate their children's parenting very highly, SAGA's research also revealed that the baby boomers believe today's parents may have let their authority fall by the wayside, with almost one in five grandparents (17%) saying they would take a stricter approach with a closer eye on bedtimes and more rigorously enforced discipline and punishment. When asked, 69% of today's parents said their parents were strict with them as a child, and 40% say they give their children more freedom than they had when they were growing up.

With 58% of children having a TV in their bedroom, and 25% having their own computer by their bedside, more than one in ten (12%) grandparents believe there is too much emphasis on technology and material goods. Grandparents say they would prefer their grandchildren to spend less time in front of the TV or on the internet and wouldn't buy them so many material things if they were parenting today's children.

However, despite these differences of opinion, most grandparents think their children are doing a good job as parents, with 91% saying they have effective parenting skills. Only 6% of grandparents think their children are ineffective as parents.

On a scale of one to ten, one-third (33%) of grandparents rated their children's parenting skills as

---

Grandmothers proved to be far more positive than grandfathers about their children's parenting ability

---

a 10. Interestingly, grandmothers proved to be far more positive than grandfathers about their children's parenting ability, with 38% of grandmothers rating them a 10 on the parenting scale, compared with just 27% of grandfathers.

Equally, today's parents think their own parents did a good job of bringing them up. Looking back at their own childhood, 95% of baby boomers' children say they appreciated what their parents did for them when they were growing up.

Andrew Goodsell, Chief Executive of SAGA, commented: 'Times have changed and today's children generally have more freedom and material goods, but this does not necessarily mean they are spoiled. Parenting skills have moved on to reflect these changes, and whilst yesterday's generation of parents would have done things differently, the vast majority are very positive about how their grandchildren are being raised.'

Note

Current parents are those aged between 16 and 49, with parents aged 50 to 65 and children aged 15 or less. 3 May 2006

- The above information is reprinted with kind permission from SAGA. Visit www.saga.co.uk for more information.

© SAGA

The cost of a child? £166,000 and rising

Raising a child from birth to 21 costs almost £166,000, according to research. The price has risen nearly 10 per cent in a year.

Parents typically spend £165,668 bringing up a child, say researchers. This is equal to £7,889 a year, £657 a month or £22 a day.

As most parents will testify, the biggest single expense is childcare which costs a total of £46,000 on average.

Cost of a child

Where the money goes	
Childcare	£46,043
Education	£37,142
Food	£15,630
Holidays	£12,109
Clothing	£12,055
Hobbies and toys	£9,369
Babysitting	£8,112
Leisure	£6,728
Pocket money	£5,170
Furniture	£2,167
Personal care	£961
Other	£10,182
Total	**£165,668**

This figure includes £30,888 in nursery costs for a child from six months to five years, assuming both parents work full time. After school care for six to 11-year-olds at 15 hours a week for 37 weeks a year, and summer holiday childcare, for four weeks a year costs £11,366.

Between the ages of 12 and 14, there is after school care and holiday care costing £3,789.

Education costs £37,000 for a state-educated child. This includes £11,570 for a child from five to 18 taking in uniform, school trips and extracurricular activities.

By Sarah Womack, Social Affairs Correspondent

Since the introduction of tuition fees, the university years have now become the most expensive.

Inner London remains the most expensive place to raise a child.

> *The cost of raising a child is up 7.8 per cent on last year's survey, more than three times the rate of inflation*

The survey by Liverpool Victoria, the friendly society, shows that the cost of raising a child is up 7.8 per cent on last year's survey, more than three times the rate of inflation, and 18 per cent higher than 2003. A breakdown of the figures shows that the average household now spends £37,142 on a child's education, which includes £25,572 on the costs of university education.

Putting a child through private schooling vastly inflates the cost of raising a child, adding £78,430.

If children go to boarding school, parents have to find a further £122,713. This means that for a child who boards at private school and goes on to university, the cost for education alone could be as high as £189,372. The total cost from birth to age 21 is £288,382.

From birth to the age of 21 the average household will spend £15,630 on a child's food, £12,109 on holidays, £12,055 on clothing, £9,369 on hobbies and toys, and £5,170 on pocket money.

Ian Cordwell, of Liverpool Victoria, said: 'Britain has a high cost of living. Education alone can be a substantial expenditure.'

25 November 2005

Parental purse problems

The parents who keep on giving

The rise of the 'adultescent' – grown-up children who still live at home with their parents – is having a major impact on mums' and dads' budgets. A new survey has found that one in three parents are spending as much as £5,000 a year for children over the age of 25.

The survey found that the two largest areas where 'adultescents' were draining the parental purse was in university education and getting on to the housing ladder.

A spokesperson for Insight Investment, which commissioned the research commented: 'At a time when empty nesters should be prioritising their own financial independence, many are finding that pressures on the parental purse strings are eating into their potential retirement pot. Increasing financial pressures such as soaring house prices and mounting student debt are unlikely to abate any time soon, so empty nesters of the future should plan ahead.'

3 April 2006

■ The above information is reprinted with kind permission from Raising Kids. For more parenting information go to www.raisingkids.co.uk.

Parental responsibility

Information from Parentline Plus

What is parental responsibility?

Parental responsibility is where an adult is responsible for the care and well-being of their child and can make important decisions about the following points:

- food;
- clothing;
- education;
- home;
- medical treatment.

Who has parental responsibility?

A married couple who have children together both automatically have parental responsibility. Parental responsibility continues after divorce.

Parental responsibility is where an adult is responsible for the care and well-being of their child

---

Mothers automatically have parental responsibility. Where the parents are not married, the unmarried father has parental responsibility if:

- his name is registered on the birth certificate – this is the case for births registered after 1 December 2003. Fathers can re-register if their names have not been placed on the birth certificate before this date;
- he later marries the mother;
- both parents have signed an authorised parental responsibility agreement;
- he obtains a parental responsibility order from the court;
- he obtains a residence order from the court;
- he becomes the child's guardian.

Others, such as grandparents and stepparents, do not have parental responsibility. They can acquire it by:

- being appointed as a guardian to care for a child if their parent dies;
- obtaining a residence order from the court for a child to live with them;
- adopting the child.

Why would someone want parental responsibility?

If you are living permanently with a child in a parental role, you may feel that you want the authority, stability and recognition. This is especially so if the other parent has no contact, or is abroad, unknown or dead.

Without parental responsibility you cannot make the decisions about a child's life, such as choice of school or religion, surname or guardian on your death.

If you are a step-parent, you cannot automatically have the child live with you on the death of a resident parent unless you have parental responsibility and so the other parent (providing that he or she has parental responsibility) will take the child.

If someone new gets parental responsibility, do others automatically lose it?

No, several people can have parental responsibility at the same time. Adoption and care proceedings are different. Parental responsibility can be lost in the case of:

- parents, where their child is adopted;
- a person having acquired parental responsibility through a court order, that order later being revoked by the court;
- a local authority with a care order and the court later revoking the care order;
- a guardian, where the court appoints another guardian.

How long does it take and what does it cost?

You can sign a parental responsibility form immediately – download the form from www.hmcourts-service.gov.uk/courtfinder/forms/c(pra)(9.01).pdf

If you have to go to court there is a duty to deal promptly with all matters concerning children and applications are treated as priority matters.

The court fees are straightforward, but if you have to go to court you should obtain legal advice and discuss fees with your solicitor.

- The above information is reprinted with kind permission from Parentline Plus. For more information, please visit the Parentline Plus website at www.parentlineplus.org.uk.

© Parentline Plus

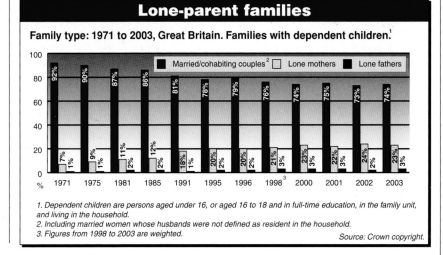

Lone-parent families

Family type: 1971 to 2003, Great Britain. Families with dependent children.[1]

Legend: Married/cohabiting couples[2] ☐ Lone mothers ■ Lone fathers

Year	Married/cohabiting couples	Lone mothers	Lone fathers
1971	92%	7%	1%
1975	90%	9%	1%
1981	87%	11%	2%
1985	86%	12%	2%
1991	81%	18%	1%
1995	78%	20%	2%
1996	79%	20%	2%
1998[3]	76%	21%	3%
2000	74%	23%	3%
2001	75%	22%	3%
2002	73%	24%	2%
2003	74%	23%	3%

1. Dependent children are persons aged under 16, or aged 16 to 18 and in full-time education, in the family unit, and living in the household.
2. Including married women whose husbands were not defined as resident in the household.
3. Figures from 1998 to 2003 are weighted.

Source: Crown copyright.

Being a parent: the basics

Information from Need2Know

Having a child can be one of the most amazing things we can do in our lives. But it can also provide us with one of our biggest challenges.

Having a child means a lifelong commitment to someone who will need your care and support for upwards of the next 16 years of your life.

Although there are 720,000 babies born every year in the UK, many people don't realise fully the effects that having a child can have

Although there are 720,000 babies born every year in the UK, many people don't realise fully the effects that having a child can have on your family, your education or career, your lifestyle and even the relationship with your partner.

Caring for a child

Some of the qualities you will need to care for a child include:

- energy – children, particularly newborn babies, can require round the clock care. You'll need to be there for them whenever they need you
- patience – whether it's your baby daughter's habit of playing with her food, or waiting for your teenage son to get home before midnight, you'll need to compromise all the while
- good time management – you will need to be able to juggle your life with the needs of your child. This is why many new parents always look tired!
- responsibility – you'll need to make sure your child gets the necessary injections, that they eat nourishing and healthy food and that they go to school.

No matter what your personal strengths are, at some point you will probably need the help of your family to bring up your children. For the majority of people, parents, brothers and sisters can provide a good support network.

Help and support

Support with benefits and housing may be available, but the level of help you can get depends on things like your age, whether you are unemployed or working, whether you have given birth and whether you are living with your partner.

For advice on what support you are able to receive as a parent, contact your local Citizens Advice Bureau or your local Jobcentre Plus office.

Giving birth to a child can seriously affect your education or career. Whether it's a dream career in hairdressing or brain surgery, you may have to put your career aspirations on hold. But just because you're young, that doesn't mean you have any fewer employment rights.

There is support with the cost of registered childcare from the Government called Care to Learn. Call 0845 600 2809 for more information. You could also try talking to a Connexions adviser on 08080 013219, who will be able to talk you through your options.

The reality of being a parent

As a parent, you will also need to make sure your child gets an education. It will be your responsibility to make sure your children go to school everyday and on time. A list of local schools in your area should be available from your local council.

As well as caring for your child, it's also important to look after your own well-being. If you can, try to spend some time on your own or socialise with friends to recharge your batteries. Or, invite your family or friends around so you can catch up with the world while keeping an eye on your child. You could also use this time to swap parenting tips with friends or family.

■ Information from Need2Know. Visit www.need2know.co.uk for more information.

© Crown copyright

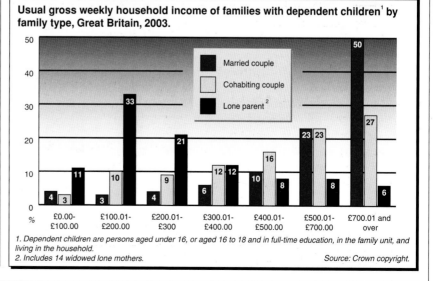

Family income

Usual gross weekly household income of families with dependent children[1] by family type, Great Britain, 2003.

Legend:
- Married couple
- Cohabiting couple
- Lone parent[2]

%	£0.00-£100.00	£100.01-£200.00	£200.01-£300	£300.01-£400.00	£400.01-£500.00	£500.01-£700.00	£700.01 and over
Married couple	4	3	4	6	10	23	50
Cohabiting couple	11	10	9	12	16	23	27
Lone parent	3	33	21	12	8	8	6

1. Dependent children are persons aged under 16, or aged 16 to 18 and in full-time education, in the family unit, and living in the household.
2. Includes 14 widowed lone mothers.

Source: Crown copyright.

Support for parents

Parents want friendly support, not professional help

A new survey out today reveals that three-quarters of parents would seek support from family, friends or neighbours, compared with less than half who would consult professional or official sources like childminders, health visitors or TV programmes.

The research was commissioned to launch the 'Real Parents' campaign to recruit volunteers to support struggling parents, launching this Mother's Day (Sunday 26th March 2006).

More than two-thirds of parents said their life was easier before having children

It's 2006 – families are geographically distant, and community networking is low. Where do you turn to for friendly parenting support? 'Real Parents' is a unique campaign to encourage people with parenting experience to become home visiting volunteers, offering emotional support and practical help to families who are struggling to cope, from volunteering charity TimeBank and national family support charity Home-Start.

Most people find being a parent of young children difficult – more than two-thirds said their life was easier before having children, one in four admitted they didn't cope easily and nearly one in five worry that other people are more competent parents. When asked what they found most difficult about being a parent of under fives, the overwhelming majority – more than a quarter – cited 'lack of sleep', while one in ten said it was 'not having enough time in the day'.

Home-Start volunteers help parents who may be struggling for many reasons; for example, with post-natal depression, multiple births, disabilities, isolation, family breakdown or through becoming parents at a young age. Clinical psychologist and TV expert, Oliver James, says:

'To offer this sort of friendly and non-judgemental support, Home-Start needs "real" parents who can relate to the difficulties faced by young families – not "super nannies" who could be intimidating.'

Kara Evans from Birmingham volunteers with Faz, who has recovered from cancer and now has a low immune system. Kara says:

'I've been helping Faz out at home because she's recovering from cancer and feels weak at times. I give practical and emotional support to Faz and her young son, who is 3½.

'We hit it off immediately. We've only known each other for 18 months but it feels like it's been years. We're very comfortable in each other's company. I don't feel like a volunteer any more – she's a mate.

'Going shopping with Faz, playing with her son while she takes a shower or just being there for a chat are all little things that really help take the pressure off.'

The survey showed an amazing 98% of people felt they had gained or developed skills as a result of being a parent. The most commonly gained assets were knowledge of health/safety/development of young children (93%), listening (90%) and patience (87%). People also said they developed practical skills like budgeting (73%) and housekeeping and cooking skills (64%).

Home-Start volunteers bring all the knowledge they've gained as parents to the families they support, helping to build the confidence of vulnerable parents and encouraging them to manage independently. In return, volunteers feel valued and the experience they gain supporting families can even help them get back to work or change careers.

Celebrity mums Natasha Hamilton and Ulrika Jonsson are supporting the campaign. Ulrika said:

'I'm backing this campaign because I know how valuable the emotional and practical support of a Home-Start volunteer could be to a parent of young children.

'Being a parent is one of the toughest jobs in the world – I've certainly had times of doubt and despair when I didn't know which way to turn. But you do get through it and the experience you gain by being a mum or dad is a brilliant asset. Why not share your skills and knowledge with another parent?

'By supporting other parents you could help give children the best possible start in life in secure and happy environments.'

The survey found that Richard Madeley and Judy Finnegan and Jamie and Jools Oliver are the celebrities British parents would most likely turn to for parenting advice or support. Each couple received over a quarter of the votes. The prime minister and his wife came a close second, with more than one in ten parents saying they would turn to them for support. They were closely followed by Sharon and Ozzy Osbourne (third); David and Victoria Beckham (fourth); Madonna and Guy Ritchie (fifth); Jordan (sixth). 'Earth mother' Angelina Jolie (seventh) gained only one-third of the votes the unorthodox Osbournes received. Atomic Kitten Kerry Katona (eighth) only managed to scoop 2% of the vote despite having been twice voted celebrity mum of the year. Model Kate Moss (ninth) gained just 1% of the vote.

To find out more about becoming a Home-Start volunteer visit www.realparents.org.uk or call 0845 601 4008 or text 07766 40 41 42.
21 March 2006

■ From a press release produced by Home-Start (www.home-start.org.uk) and TimeBank (www.realparents.org.uk). Reproduced with permission.
© Home-Start and TimeBank

Fathers aren't from Mars

Dads are becoming ever more actively involved in the lives of their children and Adam Lindsay argues they deserve greater recognition

Apparently, children whose fathers take an active role in their upbringing are more likely to do well at school and avoid getting into trouble with the police. This seemingly plain piece of common sense is the conclusion of a team of academics from the University of Lancaster, who examined 700 British and international reports spanning 20 years on the impact of fatherhood.

They found that children in Britain are likely to achieve better GCSE results if their fathers are more involved with their development. Led by Professor Charlie Lewis, the research team reported: 'In families where fathers offer kindness, care and warmth during primary school years, children are likely to do well at secondary school.'

For *Daily Mail* writers and Tory party leadership contenders, this must sound like perfect material for a sanctimonious soundbite in favour of marriage, followed, no doubt, by yet another brickbat for all those single mums. What's more, Professor Lewis says that fathers are now the main carers for children when the mothers are at work.

So maybe the publication of this report just before Fathers' Day was a bit cute, but the timing ensured it was picked up by the national media, thereby helping the good professor to achieve one of his objectives. His research aims to help extinguish the myth that fathers are remote and irrelevant to the lives of their children. At last! What a change it makes to read something that is supportive of fathers. It's also refreshing to receive acknowledgement that our role has changed and – more importantly – our approach is vastly different to that of our own fathers.

But wait: Professor Lewis also found that although the amount of time that fathers spent with their children hadn't changed in 40 years, the sharp rise in the number of working mothers meant that fathers now played a more active role in child-rearing. And this is where I think the good intentions of our friends in academia start to flounder. You see, the modern family unit depends more on the 'new nanny state' and not the new enlightened, 'hands-on' Dad, to meet the demands of raising children when both parents are working.

Children in Britain are likely to achieve better GCSE results if their fathers are more involved with their development

---

This is certainly true of many dual-parent households in London and the Home Counties. The combination of rampant house prices, the longest working hours in Europe and the drive for social equality by working mothers, necessitates a 'third parent' to look after the kids.

Hence the rise of the Eastern-European au pair, barely out of her teens, escorting the pre-school children to Wimbledon Park, or negotiating the people carrier through Hampstead to pick up little Sophie and Edmund after school. Professor Lewis's report suggests as much concluding that in 36% of dual-income families, it is the father more than any other individual who cares for the children when the mother is at work. What happens with the other 64%, I ask?

Am I sounding too negative? Only if you're feeling a twinge of guilt.

The other day my wife and I listed all our other married friends with children and found that, apart from ourselves, only two other couples out of 13 had a parent who stayed at home full-time to raise the children.

Family types and dependent children

Percentage of dependent children living in different family types, Great Britain.

	1972	1981	1992[1]	2001[1]	2003[1]
Couple familes					
1 child	16	18	18	17	17
2 children	35	41	39	38	37
3 or more children	41	29	27	25	24
Lone mother families					
1 child	2	3	4	6	6
2 children	2	4	5	7	8
3 or more children	2	3	4	5	6
Lone father families					
1 child	-	1	1	1	2
2 or more children	1	1	1	1	1

1. At spring. These estimates are not seasonally adjusted and have not been adjusted to take account of the Census 2001 results.

Source: General Household Survey, Census, Labour Force Survey, Office for National Statistics. Crown copyright.

Two others (both mothers) worked part-time, but the other eight couples had nannies. This is what I mean by the 'new nanny state'.

No fewer than 88% of boys want to be fathers when they are older, and 90% of girls want the father of their children to be caring rather than rich

---

In the old days, when three generations would live under one roof, a grandparent would often help raise the children. Nowadays, grandparents are increasingly considered a nuisance and shunted off to the nearest nursing home. A nanny is preferable to a granny, especially if she looks like Anna Kournikova. She creates a great impression with the other dads when picking up little Sophie and Edmund at the school gate!

Yes, fathers are taking on more visible and active roles with their children and that's a good thing, but I'd like to see more of it, and see greater recognition too. Professor Lewis' report helps, but if we are

doing such a great job, why is it that in a survey conducted by the charity, Fathers Direct, 91% of children aged nine to 11 still want to see more of dad? Is it because they aren't getting enough time with dad, or because they enjoy his company so much that they want more?

I'm not being naïve, but I do like to be optimistic about the future. And there are some facts I can draw on to support this faith. That same group of nine to 11-year-olds who wanted more time with dad also valued their fathers and considered the role to be important. No fewer than 88% of boys want to be fathers when they are older, and 90% of girls want the father

of their children to be caring rather than rich. More than 75% of these children also said it was OK for dad to stay at home looking after the kids while mum goes out to work. Clearly, the kids have come to terms with the concept of the 'house husband' better than today's mothers and fathers.

I am encouraged and find it fortunate that, as ever, the future of parenting lies in the hands of our children.

■ The above information is reprinted with kind permission from iVillage UK. Visit www.iVillage.co.uk for more information.
© *iVillage UK*

Styles of parenting

Information from RollerCoaster.ie

While we are all individuals and have a unique relationship with our children, researchers have identified three general styles of parenting. These three styles have been found to be associated with different behaviours and personality traits of children.

The three styles of parenting are called: authoratative, authoritarian, and permissive parenting.

Authoritative parenting style

This style of parenting is characterised by parents who allow their children quite a bit of freedom but do have clear standards of behaviour. They will reason with their children and listen to their views but will not be afraid to insist on some behaviours and will be firm in setting limits and sticking to them. They tend to have warm relationships with their children and are sensitive to their child's needs and views. They are quick to praise their child's achievements and are clear in their expectations of their child.

Authoritarian parenting style

This style of parenting is quite strict, with the child being expected to behave and the consequences of misbehaviour being harsh. The rules are enforced rigidly but are not often explained clearly or the child's wishes or opinions listened to. The emphasis is on unquestioning obedience and respect for authority. Discipline in these households tends to be harsh and punitive.

Permissive parenting style

Parents in this group allow their children to freely express themselves and do not enforce clear rules on acceptable or otherwise behaviour. They often accept or ignore bad behaviour and make few demands on their children for mature independent behaviour. Their relationship with their children is warm and accepting. When setting limits they try reasoning with their child rather than using power to assert their wishes.

■ The above information is reprinted with kind permission from RollerCoaster.ie. Visit www.rollercoaster.ie for more information.
© *RollerCoaster.ie*

The 'new man' myth

Survey shatters 'new man' myth as all talk and no nappies

One of the most comprehensive studies of family life has exploded the myth of the 'new man' who takes equal responsibility for his children.

Rather than spending more time with their offspring, today's fathers are less involved in childcare than men in the 1950s and 1960s.

Men may think they are 'new dads' who change nappies, but in fact women are taking a bigger role in children's upbringing than they used to, according to the study published by the Institute of Education.

'Highly-educated men who become dads want to spend time with their children but the reality is that they are working long hours,' said Professor Shirley Dex.

'Though they espouse a more egalitarian view they very often don't deliver because they think it would be career death.'

*By Liz Lightfoot,
Education Correspondent*

The research looked at data from cohort studies in 1958 and 1970 and compared it with the continuing millennium study, which began in 2001. It found that higher proportions of mothers now reported being mostly responsible for children.

'Overall, findings from the three studies do not support the notion of a "new dad" who spends more time with his children. In fact, they seem to suggest that fathers today are taking a slightly smaller role in childcare,' said the briefing from the Centre for Longitudinal Studies at the Institute in London.

'Middle-class parents were likely to express more egalitarian views, although this was not evident in their behaviour.'

Professor Dex, who heads the Centre, said the data showed a wide variation across the social classes in men's responsibility for childcare.

'Fathers in manual jobs are spending more time with their children in all three studies. Some are organising their shifts to fit in with working mothers.'

The perception among middle-class men that they were more involved in their children might stem from the fact that they were much more likely to be present at the birth than in the past, she said.

The study showed that 46 per cent of fathers were reported to play an equal part in parenting in 1958, dropping to 39 per cent in 1970.

Only just over one-fifth of men today were satisfied with the number of hours they felt they could spend with their families.

30 November 2005

Full-time fathers

The work-life balance debate

Daddy daycare

There's a certain image of stay-at-home dads – children with unbrushed hair, wearing odd socks and ankleswinger trousers – that is somewhat unfair. Fathers have different priorities when it comes to looking after children. There's no doubt mums are more likely to indulge their love of dressing the dolly, but it's hardly a key indicator of quality care. It's a minor point, but it highlights a core issue. A lot of the success of a father as main carer hinges on whether or not the mother can surrender control and leave her partner to get on with the job.

Sarah is a solicitor and works full time while husband Mike looks after their children, Warwick, two and baby Nathaniel, two months. The couple planned that Mike would be the main carer before their first child was born. Like most parents, Mike didn't have any experience, he's learned on the job. Does he have a

> *There's a certain image of stay-at-home dads – children with unbrushed hair, wearing odd socks and ankleswinger trousers – that is somewhat unfair*

network of mum or dad friends, how does he manage his day?

'I try to keep in touch with one or two mums I met at the National Childbirth Trust (NCT) couples' antenatal classes. Warwick and I go to TJ's gymnastics, gymboree and Spanish together. There are a few other dads, about one in 20. People are generally friendly, but we don't tend to socialise outside the classes. There is a group of stay-at-home dads who meet in Wimbledon Park. I went to a few meetings but they tended to come from quite a broad area, travelling quite a distance.'

So, does Mike feel isolated?

'No, I muddle along and Warwick keeps me quite busy. We go to the park and one o'clock clubs. We walk the dog on the common. By the time Warwick has his sleep, we've sorted out mealtimes and gone to a class, there's not much of the day left.'

Full-time father, two tiny children, and a dog? Nobody could keep on top of the housework with that much going on, surely?

Mike admits, 'I do the housework, but not as much as my wife would like, and we have a cleaner. My wife is probably more houseproud than me, but you have to let things slide a little bit while the children are so young.'

So in Mike's opinion, what are the differences between care given by the father or mother? What are the benefits?

'I think Warwick is a lot calmer than other boys. He's a good sport and relaxed most of the time. There's a lot of pressure on mums, the heat is on for them to be perfect. I'm not affected by that and I can go my own way a bit because there's not a stereotype father figure that I've got to live up to. I plough my own furrow.'

Presumably, in the future Mike will go back to work at some point. But he doesn't seem to be worried about the loss of earnings and career setback that most female returners experience.

'Little Nat is only small and I'll certainly be here with him until he starts school. I have the advantage that I had more or less decided that I wouldn't be doing what I used to do any more. When I go back I'll be starting over, so I'm not going to lose too much career-wise.'

Alan Charlton is the author of *Chips, Videos and Alcohol*, a new survival guide for daycare daddies. He has been at home since the birth of his first child, 13 years ago.

'After we got married we talked about starting a family, and in that conversation was who, when and how do we look after this baby? Purely on a financial basis, I put myself forward to stay at home. My wife's prospects were better than mine and with the long hours she works, it was clear someone needed to be there to take the reins. I jumped in at the deep end.'

Do people treat full-time fathers differently? Was it easy to make friends?

'We went to the NCT group before the birth, but afterwards it tails off. I'd go round for coffee, but it feels uncomfortable as a man. I was new to it and unsure how to put my point across. I'm sitting in the corner drinking tea and they're talking about nipple soreness – sorry, I can't sympathise with that one! When a

mother walks out with a pushchair, people say hello and want to look at the baby. When it's a man, people don't particularly take an interest. They assume mum is at the doctor, or you're separated and it's your turn to look after the baby. Apart from the girls on the checkout, people didn't talk to me.'

After the birth of Alan's second child, now nine, he hooked up with another dad.

'The local clinic contacted me and said there was interest in getting a fathers group together. On the day, only one chap turned up. We used to meet at the pub once a week, no children, and the last thing we would talk about was babies. We'd bitch about problems with our partners. It was very therapeutic.'

For some reason I had always thought that the feeling of isolation when you're at home with a new baby, the loss of confidence, was a hormonal thing peculiar to mothers. Alan's experience indicates otherwise,

'I did lose my confidence for a bit, you become a bit of a brain-dead guppy. You don't appreciate the job you're doing.'

It's comforting to learn that those feelings have nothing to do with the physical changes a mother undergoes, it is just a normal reaction to the sheer hard work of looking after a baby. Men and women are equally susceptible.

Of course, a lot has changed in 13 years. In April the new Fatherhood Quality Mark was launched, requiring all children's services to be more dad-friendly. It means local authorities, primary care trusts and children's services have to provide information targeted to fathers. Hopefully this will make it easier for stay-at-home dads to feel connected and valued.

So what advice does Alan have for other parents considering a similar arrangement? What would he do differently?

'Fathers should read my book for a real picture of what it's like, warts and all. I don't care how much you discuss it. When the baby comes into your life, it's not going to work the way you think. One of you will have to give in and be the primary carer, make the big decisions and the other person fit in around it.

'Try and keep some work aspect to your life, just to get you out of the routine of nappies and sick. It gives you an extra £30 in your pocket, which feels marvellous when it's your money. It's alright to say that now, but at the time I don't think I could have coped with working. I was very protective of the baby and very absorbed in it. If you have the option of a grandparent looking after the child, fantastic. I don't think parents in that situation understand how lucky they are!'

Alan Charlton's book *Chips, Videos and Alcohol: a Father's Guide to Survival* (New Holland Publishers, £7.99) is out now.

Dad facts

- Pre-schoolers who spend time playing with their dads are more sociable when they enter nursery school.
- Involvement of dads with children aged 7 to 11 predicts success in exams aged 16.
- Where dads are involved before the age of 11, children are less likely to have a criminal record by the time they are 21.

Source: www.fathersdirect.com

- The above information is reprinted with kind permission from Families. Visit www.familiesonline.co.uk for more information.

© Families

1 in 3 fathers work 48+ hours a week

Information from the Office for National Statistics (ONS)

Most dependent children (80 per cent) live with their father, but one in 50 children live only with their father. Changes in family life mean that some fathers may be non-married, no-longer married or remarried; they may be a biological or a social father.

Fathers with dependent children are more likely to be employed and to work longer hours than men without. Ninety per cent of fathers are in employment compared with 74 per cent of working-age men without dependent children. Fathers in full-time employment work for 47 hours every week on average compared with 40 hours by mothers working full time. The 'long hours culture' particularly affects fathers – one-third work over 48 hours a week.

Ninety per cent of fathers are in employment compared with 74 per cent of working-age men without dependent children

---

Many working fathers also help out with childcare. On average, fathers working full-time spent one hour on weekdays and 40 minutes more on weekend days on childcare. The younger the child, the more time fathers spent on such activities. This time spent with their children was divided equally between caring and reading, playing and talking with children.

But most of the dirty work is still done by mothers. Almost four in 10 fathers with babies report changing nappies more than once a day, while

one in 11 report never changing nappies. At 2 1/2 hours each weekend day, mothers spend more than double the amount of time than fathers on cooking, cleaning and tidying (fathers spend 1 hour 10 minutes).

Fathers pull their weight in other ways, by spending one hour on weekend days doing construction jobs, repairs, gardening and looking after pets. This is double the time spent by mothers on these tasks at 30 minutes.

Father's Day 2006 is on 18 June. Market research carried out on behalf of the greetings card industry showed

that last year 23 million Father's Day cards were sent in the UK, at a cost of £32 million.

Sources
- *Social Trends 36*, ONS, 2006
- *Labour Market Trends*, ONS, July 2005 – Labour Force Survey 2004
- *Parenting in the UK*, ESRC – Website – Millennium Cohort Study First Survey 2001-2003
- *Time Use and Childcare*, Equal Opportunities Commission, January 2005 – Time Use 2000, ONS
- Greetings card industry figures were provided by Greeting Card Association, courtesy of Harris Interactive.

16 June 2006

- The above information is re-printed with kind permission from the Office for National Statistics. Visit www.statistics.gov.uk for more information.

© Crown copyright

100-hour-a-week women

It's official! Being a mum is the 'hardest working profession in Europe', according to a new report. So what's the reaction on the shop floor? By Lynette Lowthian

Mums work harder than anyone else, putting in at least 100 hours each week in cleaning, childcare, doing the school run and keeping on top of the laundry. This is more than double the 43.6-hour working week of the average British worker – not forgetting that this is already the highest number of working hours in Europe.

For 40 per cent of the women in the survey, the working day doesn't end until 9pm, and one-third sleep less than six hours a night

A new survey for fabric conditioner Comfort, which looked at the lives of more than 1,000 British women, uncovers a picture of relentlessly busy days. For 40 per cent of the women in the survey,

100-hour-a-week women	
Who knows where the time goes?	
Childcare	4
Work/paid employment	25
Travelling (including school run)	5
Washing up/loading dishwasher	5
Laundry	6
Cleaning and dusting	6
Vacuuming	3
Cooking	9
Total	**100**

the working day doesn't end until 9pm, and one-third sleep less than six hours a night. There is no let-up at weekends: one in three women say they are as busy then as they are during the week.

The long hours mean that women have precious little, or no time, to call their own. Average daily 'me time' is just one hour. More than half (54 per cent) of the women say they have given up wearing make-up.

So just what are they doing with their time (as if we needed to ask the question!)? It's taken up with cleaning, laundering, childcare, the school run – and often part-time work on top. In London, an average seven hours a week is devoted to the school run.

Meanwhile, mums in the West Midlands don't just get out the iron – they spent a horrific 24 hours a week pushing it back and forth across the ironing board!

And just in case the business fraternity are about to scoff at the notion that this is 'real' work, mums in the survey point out that this sort of labour is often physical, relentless, goes unnoticed and is unpaid.

■ Reproduced by permission of *Right Start* magazine. Visit www. rightstartmagazine.co.uk for more information.

© *Right Start*

Are you a six per center?

Only six in 100 mothers with young families want to work full-time

A new survey out today presents us with the not altogether surprising statistic that most mums with young children would prefer not to work full-time. *Prima* magazine, who polled 1,000 women, found that just 6% wanted to work full-time. 50% wanted to mix work and childcare, while 26% wanted to be stay-at-home mothers.

Maire Fahey, editor of *Prima*, said: 'In the 1980s, we thought we could have it all and aspired to high-flying careers and happy families. But the cracks are starting to show. Family life is suffering and something has got to give. And for most women, our survey shows that it is their career that is going to go.'
5 January 2006

■ The above information is reprinted with kind permission from Raising Kids. For more parenting information go to www.raisingkids.co.uk.
© *Raising Kids*

Kid gloves

Are we over-protective of our children? By Claire Benians

How can parents strike the right balance between sensible safety precautions and allowing children to make their own discoveries of the environment they live in?

With blanket media coverage of such tragic events as the disappearance and murder of young girls like Holly Wells and Jessica Chapman in 2002, today's parents can be forgiven for keeping their children close by at all times. Many parents drive their children to the school gates and see them enter the grounds rather than let them walk or cycle to school. And in the home, parents are encouraged – if not expected – to buy a huge number of safety devices to keep curiosity at bay. Everything from cupboard doors and stairs to video machines can be 'child-proofed'.

But could these good intentions ultimately be sending the wrong message to today's children? How can parents strike the right balance between sensible precautions – such as road safety awareness – and allowing children to make their own discoveries about the environment they live in?

Factbox

- Fewer than three children in every million in Britain is at risk from being murdered.
- More than 200 children per million are killed on our roads each year.
- On average, children walk one-fifth less than they used to 20 years ago.
- An estimated 8.5% of six-year-olds in Britain are considered obese.
- Calories burnt in weekly school travel by bicycle or on foot exceed those burnt in two hours of PE per week, the recommended requirement for pupils (Roger Mackett, University College London).

Helpful tots?

So when should parents start agreeing to let their children do things alone? Most children will want to start asserting their independence from quite a young age and there are lots of ways parents can encourage this without putting their child at risk.

For pre-schoolers, the home is the easiest place to start. Zo, who lives in Barnes, took her cue from her son. 'From around age three or so, Michael was very keen to help me stack the dishwasher. Rather than say no, I felt it was important to let him get more involved around the home – fully supervised to avoid accidents of course.'

> *Fewer than three children in every million in Britain is at risk from being murdered*

The Montessori teaching method advocates a similar approach for young children. According to Montessori Centre International, children can 'learn to manage their own clothes using dressing frames to practise buttons, zips and bows. They are also shown how to care for their classroom, using child-sized brushes and dusters. Developing practical skills – like pouring drinks from a jug and laying tables – and social skills with friends and teachers, enable them to feel capable, self-reliant members of the community.'

Away from home

However, for the majority of parents, what happens to their children outside the home causes the most angst. Road safety as well as the much-feared lurking stranger are at the heart of this anxiety.

There are no hard-and-fast rules about when it is safe to start allowing a child to undertake these trips on their own. A lot will depend on the child's confidence, on whether they live in a rural or urban setting and on the attitude of parents.

Catherine, who lives in Balham, is mother of a 10-year-old son and an eight-year-old daughter. Whilst she

recognises that her son is desperate to cycle on his own locally and allows him to make short trips, Catherine finds it hard not to worry. As she explains, 'I recently let Mark pop to the local shop to buy lemon curd for a recipe we were making. After half an hour he still hadn't returned and I started to panic. But he reappeared with a Sainsbury's bag – he had tried two local shops with no luck and thought he'd go to the supermarket instead!'

In terms of when it is appropriate for children to undertake short trips on their own, Catherine waited until her children were almost eight before allowing them to do so. And even then, she made sure she could see them cross a busy road. According to the 'What to Expect' series of parenting books, 'it won't be until about age ten… that a child will be able to safely cross a busy street by himself.'

On Your Bike…

Cycling poses particular challenges in terms of safety. Not only can children travel quite significant distances by bicycle, they must also have good road awareness to keep out of trouble.

Sustrans, a charity which works on projects to encourage people to walk and cycle, has some useful advice: 'Parents are likely to want to accompany younger children who are cycling. For older children who can cycle to school on their own, parents might still like to check out local routes to establish the safest way to go.'

Sustrans also recommends that any child cycling regularly undertakes cycle training. The old Cycling Proficiency Scheme has been replaced by a three-tier National Standard for Cycle Training. Children of any age can do the training, Level 1 being the most basic.

Live a little!

Encouraging children to be self-reliant and confident in their dealings with the world is no easy task. But with sensible supervision and precautions backed up with hard and fast rules about what is and isn't acceptable behaviour from others, parents can feel more comfortable about relaxing their grip a little!

As the Suzy Lamplugh Trust puts it: 'There is no doubt that it can be a dangerous world but the dangers must be kept in proportion. Nobody wants children to be so molly-coddled that they cannot live their lives to the full. Life is for living and one of the best gifts you can give a child is the knowledge and confidence to do so as safely as possible.'
1 January 2006

■ Information from Families. Visit www.familiesonline.co.uk for more information.

© Families

When parents won't let go

You've left the family nest, but when are they going to treat you like an adult? We look at how to cope when your folks are just too in-your-face

The scenario

For some, leaving home doesn't mark the beginning of an independent life. It's more like an escape bid that never really comes off. From unexpected calls to unwanted guidance and guilt

---

No family agrees on everything. In many ways, a difference of opinion is a healthy thing, especially between you and a parent

---

trips, some parents really know how to make life a misery. They probably don't mean it, of course, but if it's becoming a problem then it needs to be sorted.

Often, a good starting point is to identify how they're doing your head in, and why. So, here's how they misbehave according to type.

Parental problem 1: disapproval

No family agrees on everything. In many ways, a difference of opinion is a healthy thing, especially between you and a parent. It can promote a constructive debate, or highlight individual strengths. As long as it's conducted with respect and sensitivity, then your relationship is likely to thrive. In many cases, however, one parent's values can be so rigid that anything you say or do can be met with pursed lips and a heavy silence. I had the most beautiful furniture in

my bedroom,' says Zella, 20, whose parents expressed their disapproval more directly. Admittedly it was bondage stuff, a whipping post and a bondage chair, but they just couldn't handle it and leapt to all kinds of conclusions.'
Solution
It doesn't matter how many times you tell them that you can make responsible decisions for yourself,

you can't beat showing them. It might mean toughing it out while you prove that you know what you're doing, but ultimately your welfare is what drives them to have their say. If they can see you're in control of your life, they should begin to leave you alone.

It's easy to say that parents love their children equally, but the fact is such love can be displayed in ways that leave you feeling overshadowed

---

Parental problem 2: emotional blackmail

A parent's love is unconditional. Unless, that is, you're not co-operating when it comes to bending to their will. The 'family loyalty' card is very easy to play, and we've all been guilty of it in some shape or form, so try not to see red. You might be faced with a sense that you've let them down, or a constant trickle of repeat requests that can't fail to wear you down.
Solution
There's nothing more irritating than knowing you're being manipulated. Yes, you do need to stand up to it. The key is to do so without escalating the

problem. In this situation, it's often best to agree to whatever you're being asked to do, but then raise the bigger issue at a time when you're both calm and collected. If you can avoid the problem, you'll get results.

Parental problem 3: favouritism

It's easy to say that parents love their children equally, but the fact is such love can be displayed in ways that leave you feeling overshadowed. It might be a form of emotional blackmail, in order to get you to comply, but it can also eat into other aspects of your life.
Solution
You might find the best person to approach about this isn't the offending parent, but the sibling who's earned their special attention. If they aren't already aware of what's happening, hopefully you'll get their support and understanding. You're adults, after all. What's more, a quiet word from them could well wake up your mum or dad to the fact that you don't deserve this kind of treatment.

Parental problem 4: sulking

The first time I said I had other plans for Christmas,' recalls Lise, 22, Mum's voice just went shrill and I knew I had messed up. She wouldn't admit it was a problem, but it left me feeling really guilty.'
Solution
Be big about this. Swallow your pride and talk the issue through with them

– preferably face-to-face. Don't feel obliged to apologise for something you're not sorry about, but ask them to look at the bigger picture. The last thing that either of you want is to allow a small fallout to grow into a long-term stand off in which you're effectively divorced from your parents.

Parental problem 5: phone bothering

Only you can say how often you like to stay in touch with a parent. It might be every day, once a week or less than that. What matters is that you're both happy with the frequency, and know a good time to call. For example, not before the alarm clock goes off, or half a dozen times in the same evening.
Solution
If you've made it clear that calling in the morning or at work is not good for you, consider letting your answer machine shield all calls for a while. They'll soon get the (unspoken) message. Alternatively, for repeat offenders, make the effort to call them at a convenient time during the day, and cover every subject then. If they're in the habit of ringing back straight away, don't pick up the phone. It may be blunt, but you need boundaries.

■ The above information is re-printed with kind permission from TheSite.org. Visit www.thesite.org for more information.

© TheSite.org

This house is a manipulation-free zone

Parents of teenagers: 'are we failing as parents?'

Parents of teenagers feel they are failing as parents according to a new report by charity Parentline Plus

Parents talk about having little or no influence over their teenagers and are deeply worried about such issues as binge drinking, drugs, peer pressure and early sexual activity.

The report, called *The Highs and Lows: Parenting Teenagers*, reveals that problems are starting earlier than the teenage years for lots of families – shocked by the sudden changes of mood in their child. Many talk of having to deal with a 'stranger' in the house.

'Every teenager is different. We have one who has been so lovely all his school life – now he is 13 he is a monster and I cannot identify him as my son,' one parent told the charity.

Parents can feel a sense of loss as their children grow up and completely out of their depth as their children begin breaking away from the comfort zone of their family

---

Parents can feel a sense of loss as their children grow up and completely out of their depth as their children begin breaking away from the comfort zone of their family. This often means experimenting with risk and ignoring the boundaries traditionally set by their parents.

To help those parents who are feeling they have nowhere to turn, the charity has now launched a new campaign, 'Talking Teens', to tackle these issues and has drawn up a list of recommendations to help families through these often difficult years.

Parentline~plus~

These include renewing its call for more support for parents of teenagers with families feeling it is their right to ask for support when they need it.

'It is clear from our work with parents of teenagers that they often feel helpless in being unable to deal with their own anxieties and the difficulties presented by their teenagers,' said Dorit Braun, Chief Executive of Parentline Plus.

'The good news is that there is light at the end of the tunnel, and parents can be reassured by all the evidence which shows that parents and teenagers get through this stage relatively unscathed, without affecting their fundamental relationship.'

Parents of teenagers are one of the largest groups to use Parentline Plus services – accounting for nearly 50% of all calls to the helpline – with parents' groups for teenagers being constantly in demand.

The launch of the report follows various consultations with parents including a survey on the Parentline Plus website, where parents of teenagers were asked to share their experiences and tell their stories. After just three weeks, the charity received over 100 long and passionate stories.

These include: 'My eldest daughter has changed from a loving girl into a monster! She is drinking, stealing money from me, smoking and hanging around with a bad crowd. You cannot communicate with her at the moment because everything I say she takes as a personal attack and tells me I'm ruining her life! I know I probably did all these things too but I did always respect my mum and wouldn't talk back like she does. How do you get that respect back?'

What parents tell us – key findings

- Worries about early sexual activity continue to concern parents.

82% of parents raising the issue are worried about young people aged 13 to 15 with 79% about girls. Parents were also concerned about lying and the negative influence of peers.

- Binge drinking, particularly amongst girls aged 13 to 15, is another big worry for parents. They are concerned about the link between being out of control because of drinking too much with dangerous situations and unprotected sex.
- Drug use scares parents. They tell us they do not feel they understand enough about the risks and, for example, the continual arguments about the declassification of cannabis. Calls to our helpline about drug abuse are mainly about boys aged 13 to 19.

Parents and carers, and society as a whole, need to accept that parenting can be challenging and often difficult and that seeking help is not about failure

---

The majority of concerns are about the behaviour and attitudes of younger teens, with over 31% of all calls to the charity's helpline being about young people aged between 13 and 15.

'It is important to stress that where parents have the confidence to talk, listen, negotiate and set boundaries with their teenager, there is change, and with that change comes mutual respect within the family and within the community,' added Dorit.

This is reinforced by the comment of another parent, who said: 'We have been through every trauma imaginable with our 16-year-old daughter and have come through the other end! We have found communication (calmly) to be absolutely vital. So we have weekly family council to discuss good or bad things. You'd be amazed what comes up. Everyone has their turn

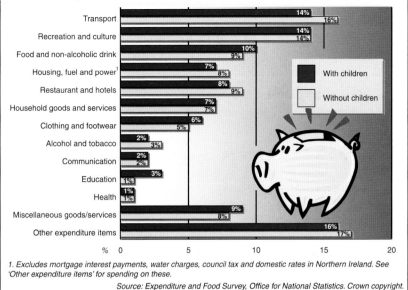

Household expenditure of parents

Household expenditure of couples with and without children, 2002-2003, UK.

Category	With children	Without children
Transport	14%	16%
Recreation and culture	14%	14%
Food and non-alcoholic drink	10%	9%
Housing, fuel and power[1]	7%	8%
Restaurant and hotels	8%	9%
Household goods and services	7%	7%
Clothing and footwear	6%	5%
Alcohol and tobacco	2%	3%
Communication	2%	2%
Education	3%	1%
Health	1%	1%
Miscellaneous goods/services	9%	8%
Other expenditure items	16%	17%

1. *Excludes mortgage interest payments, water charges, council tax and domestic rates in Northern Ireland. See 'Other expenditure items' for spending on these.*

Source: Expenditure and Food Survey, Office for National Statistics. Crown copyright.

to speak and no shouting is allowed. This seems to be the main thing that keeps our family working and living together.'

The campaign is being supported by celebrity mum Janet Ellis, who says: 'I always imagined that by the time my children hit the teenage years it would be easier. But I soon came to realise teens need you as much as younger children, if not more, just in a different way. One minute you can feel exhilarated and the next frustrated by them, but in the midst of despair it is worth holding onto the fact that you do get through the teenage years and your relationship gets stronger and stronger.'

Key recommendations

- Parents and carers, and society as a whole, need to accept that parenting can be challenging and often difficult and that seeking help is not about failure. Families need to feel it is their right to ask for support.
- More family support services on the ground, with sustained investment in their development and take up on a national, regional and local basis. Parents need to build on their communication skills, self-esteem, confidence, understanding, listening and hearing – giving them the confidence to tackle potential problems early on.
- More family support with parents

and carers of children aged 10 to 12, which would enable them to learn from others and to share experiences.

- Parents need to know the facts: they need more access to the real picture – whether it is the average age of first sexual activity or the level of drug-taking at 15, for example. Armed with accurate and appropriate knowledge, parents will stop feeling out of the picture or old-fashioned and this in turn will enhance communication with their teenagers.
- A need for more father-focused support. Fathers want help and support too.
- Schools must actively engage with families, focusing on the transition to secondary, More face to face supportive and community-orientated meeting and events can improve the level of trust between parent and school.
- It is important that schools and staff are equipped to signpost families of teenagers to sources of help.

25 April 2006

- The above information is re-printed with kind permission from Parentline Plus. Visit www. parentlineplus.org.uk for more information.

© *Parentline Plus*

Family life: the basics

Most people at some point experience arguments and disagreements within the family and many view this as part of growing up

Sibling trouble

Tension between brothers and sisters is quite common among families. It's quite normal for arguments to kick off over the simplest of things. While growing up, people can become very protective of their own private space in the family house and going into another brother or sister's bedroom can sometimes cause all hell to break loose.

Falling out with parents

It's almost a tradition that young people don't always see eye-to-eye with their parents or carers. Like with brothers and sisters, many arguments with parents can start because of disagreements over territory in the house, like needing to be alone sometimes. Rows also happen when people in families get cross over who should do which and how many of the household tasks, or looking after younger siblings.

But tensions can also arise when children in the family begin to become more independent from their parents. Having cared for their children for many years, parents can suddenly find that their children go out unannounced to socialise with friends they might not even know. Understandably, this can be a bit of shock.

People that live with one parent can also sometimes argue with the parent they don't live with. Sometimes people can resent the absent parent because they felt that they 'abandoned' them or ran away from their child.

If arguments with your parents, carers or family are getting you down, tell them. If you explain that you are not happy that the family is not getting on, they should at least listen to you. Sometimes the argument is over rules and discipline. Do think about why these rules are there in the first place, and then try to negotiate with your parents to give you more freedom by showing that you act responsibly and that they can trust you. If that doesn't work, try talking to a grandparent, aunt, uncle or cousin, or a good friend about it. Your friend might be in the same situation as you and be able to give you advice.

It's almost a tradition that young people don't always see eye-to-eye with their parents or carers

---

Some schools run peer support or mentoring schemes, which encourage pupils to support one another.

Domestic violence

Although arguing with parents or carers is something a lot of us take for granted, family life can become a source of real distress and misery for some people.

No matter how much they try to compromise with their parents, young people can sometimes suffer from violence or physical abuse.

If you feel your situation at home is becoming too stressful and you don't know what to do, try to talk it over with a friend, or with an adult that you trust, such as a teacher. However some adults, including teachers, may have to pass on information to the police or social services if they are concerned about your safety. You can always get in touch with an organisation which offers confidential advice and support.

■ The above information is reprinted with kind permission from Need2Know. Visit www.need2know.co.uk for more information.

© Crown copyright

Kids? We can't afford them!

Why Britain's families are shrinking in size

A new survey suggests that the cost of living and bringing up kids is causing British families to shrink in size. Research conducted by the Skipton Building Society found that the average family today has 1.3 children – almost half that of a generation ago.

One in five couples surveyed said that they had come to the decision not to have children at all. More than one-third of those said it was because they were unwilling to compromise their lifestyle, while a further 15 per cent were put off by the cost.

'The fact that a fifth of the UK's adults are choosing to remain childless sends a strong message about modern life and the pressures it brings – particularly financially,' said a spokesperson for the Skipton. 'There are a lot of factors contributing to this, including consumer debt, pension shortfalls and rising house prices, all of which have led many people to choose to enjoy the lifestyle they have instead of adding more pressure with the cost of bringing up a child.

'What's particularly unfortunate though is the number of people who wish to have a family but are being forced to delay doing so for purely monetary reasons.'

April 10 2006

■ The above information is reprinted with kind permission from Raising Kids. For more parenting information go to www.raisingkids.co.uk.

© Raising Kids

Friends are the new family

You're more likely to eat together, spend time together, holiday together and pull Xmas crackers. Friends are the new family, but why, and when did it all change?

Why?

- Keeping parents' approval: as teenagers, we are still actively seeking our parents' approval and do not want to come across as childish. Because of this, adolescents are more likely to be open with friends than their parents, discussing such issues as dating, sexuality, personal experiences, and common interests. In fact, according to a report by Dunn and Deater-Deckard in 2001, 79% of children confide their problems in their mates and not their parents.

> *Friendships are based on mutual voluntary ties between those on an equal footing, whereas we are tied by blood to our relatives*

- Equality: friendships are based on mutual voluntary ties between those on an equal footing, whereas we are tied by blood to our relatives, and our roles within the family.
- 'Blush factor': it is also often less embarrassing to talk to friends than parents, who are frankly too wrinkly to know, aren't they?
- Time: since adolescents spend twice as much time with peers than with parents, peer groups have recently been shown to provide surrogate family support.
- Smaller families: we have less children today, often opting for just one or two. Friendships fill the roles of brothers and sisters we never had.

When did it all change?

Friends has been a massive hit worldwide, partly because it plays on

the new importance of friends today, and their role as a second family. However, there wasn't a sudden change in the role of our families – we have gradually moved away from families living, working and playing together in small villages to the scattered-across-the-world model we have today.

As it became more commonplace for women to work rather than staying home with the kids, the whole family structure changed. Relationships and careers pushed family members out across the globe, leaving reunions and communications few and far between.

Our families are left scattered all over the place, placing friends, who are usually closer in proximity, as the prime people we spend our time with and confide in. That's not to say we don't rate our family as important, just that we now have less day-to-day contact with them, instead turning to our friends for close emotional support, and indeed including our friends in our wider circle of family.

Our fragmented lives are much more stressful than previous generations, placing a higher concern with keeping up connections. This may also explain the recent fad for reunions amongst old school friends – because we are less likely to stay in our hometown, we quickly lose touch with old friends.

Life is now about the individual and the temporary. Jobs are no longer for life, marriages and long-term relationships are no longer forever and so in their place has come the one constant – our friends, those that had always been there for us. Friendships hold the hope that they will last forever, succeeding where love fails. They'll be there for life.

- The above information is reprinted with kind permission from TheSite.org. Visit www.thesite.org for more information.

© *TheSite.org*

British family life

. . . but not as we know it

Latest research from MINTEL finds that as many as 35% of British parents[1] now live as a 'non-traditional' family unit, because they are single parents (19%) or because they have children from previous relationships (16%) living with them. This means that today around five million British parents have a 'non-traditional' family life. The remaining two-thirds (65%) of parents are 'traditional' married or cohabiting couples, living with children only from this current relationship.

The research from this report, MINTEL's first major study into the make-up of British families, finds that parents of 'non-traditional' families are more likely to suffer the financial strains of running a household. Today, almost three in ten (27%) parents in 'non-traditional' families worry about paying the bills, compared to just 16% of those in 'traditional' families. And again when it comes to outstanding debt, such as mortgages and loans, those in 'non-traditional' families (20%) are

more likely than those in 'traditional' families (16%) to worry about the amount they owe.

Time too is cause for concern. While just 35% of parents in 'traditional' families 'do not have as much time as they would like to spend doing things for themselves', this rises to as many as 42% of parents in 'non-traditional' families, which may be a result of the varying demands of children from different relationships.

'Family life has changed dramatically in recent years, and many of the changes have led to extra stresses and strains for both parents and children. The rising divorce rate, coupled with the growing trend

for serial monogamy, can mean that family structures can be very complicated, with children from several relationships being involved in stepfamilies. While these 'new extended families' can bring benefits, the problems of amalgamating two or more families into one can also be a source of tension and conflict,' comments Angela Hughes, Consumer Research Manager at MINTEL.

As many as 35% of British parents now live as a 'non-traditional' family unit, because they are single parents (19%) or because they have children from previous relationships (16%) living with them

When it comes to bringing up the children, it is those couples who have children from outside their present relationship who tend to struggle the most. Indeed, one in four (24%) adults in a 'traditional' family say that 'they do not always agree with their partner on how to bring up their children', but this rises to some three in ten (31%) amongst 'non-traditional' couples. And while some 17% of parents in a 'traditional' family say that 'their children cause frequent arguments at home', this rises to almost one in four (23%) amongst those in 'non-traditional' couples.

Singly responsible

Amongst British parents aged 16 to 24 years old, almost half (48%) live in a 'non-traditional' family, as

two in five (38%) are single parents and a further 10%, although living with a partner, have children from previous relationships. What is more, a staggering 51% of British mothers in this age group are single mums, which is in stark contrast to the mere 1% of all fathers aged under 35 who are bringing up their children alone.

'Levels of separation and divorce mean that the number of "non-traditional" families will remain high'

But age is not the greatest divider, socio-economic group is. Today, fewer than one in five (18%) parents from the more affluent AB socio-economic group live in a 'non-traditional' family. But amongst those parents in the E socio-economic group, who are dependent on state benefits, as many as 70% live in a 'non-traditional' family, making them more than twice as likely to be in a 'non-traditional' family than a 'traditional' one.

'Levels of separation and divorce mean that the number of "non-traditional" families will remain high. Organisations catering for families will increasingly need to ensure that any "family" deal offerings are flexible in their definition and appropriate for the growing number of "non-traditional" arrangements

such as single parents, weekend fathers and children looked after by grandparents,' explains Angela Hughes.

The great (parental) escape
The strains of family life are reflected in the fact that parents yearn for some time to themselves, with almost a quarter seeking leisure time or a holiday without the kids in tow.

Interestingly, despite the stereotype of the harassed father 'escaping' to the office, twice as many working mothers (30%) as working fathers (16%) admit that 'going out to work gives them valuable time away from family life'.

What is more, almost one in five (17%) working mothers 'would prefer to work more hours but can't because of family commitments' – twice the proportion of men who feel this way.

'The research indicates that there may be a big shift in the way fathers and mothers view their respective positions in terms of work and career, especially in the case of mothers who

work full time. Indeed the extent to which mothers now see themselves as breadwinners is indicated by the fact that men and women are equally likely to say they worry about not earning enough for the kind of lifestyle they would like to lead,' comments Angela Hughes.

MINTEL's research also confirms the fact that paid work can have a detrimental effect on family life, especially for working fathers, and full-time working mothers. These two groups are equally likely to say that their 'family life often suffers because of their paid work' – 26% in each case, compared with 13% of mothers who only work part-time.

Notes
1. Adults with own children under 18 in their households.

About MINTEL
MINTEL is a worldwide leader of competitive media, product and consumer intelligence. For more than 35 years, MINTEL has provided key insight into leading global trends. With offices in Chicago, London, Belfast and Sydney, MINTEL's innovative product line provides unique data that has a direct impact on client success. For more information on MINTEL, please visit their website at www.mintel.com. *July 2005*

■ The above information is reprinted with kind permission from MINTEL. Visit www.mintel.com for more information.

© MINTEL

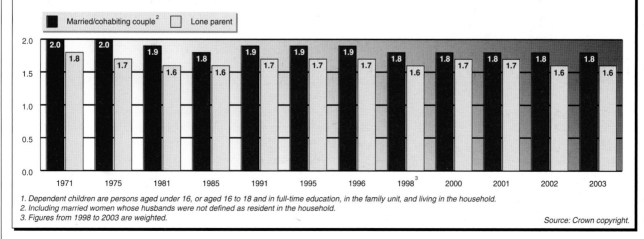

Number of dependent children by family type

Average (mean) number of dependent children[1] by family type: 1971 to 2003, Great Britain. Familes with dependent children.

Legend: ■ Married/cohabiting couple[2] □ Lone parent

	1971	1975	1981	1985	1991	1995	1996	1998[3]	2000	2001	2002	2003
Married/cohabiting couple	2.0	2.0	1.9	1.8	1.9	1.9	1.9	1.8	1.8	1.8	1.8	1.8
Lone parent	1.8	1.7	1.6	1.6	1.7	1.7	1.7	1.6	1.7	1.7	1.6	1.6

1. Dependent children are persons aged under 16, or aged 16 to 18 and in full-time education, in the family unit, and living in the household.
2. Including married women whose husbands were not defined as resident in the household.
3. Figures from 1998 to 2003 are weighted.

Source: Crown copyright.

Majority of births will soon be out of wedlock

Half of all babies will be born to unmarried mothers by 2012 if present trends continue, says new research that suggests the rapid erosion of moral and religious taboos.

Moreover, fewer than half of families will consist of married couples and up to one-third could be lone parents, said Dr Peter Brierley, a former government statistician now specialising in religious trends.

Dr Brierley's projections followed the publication of official figures yesterday showing that the number of births outside marriage has almost quadrupled in recent decades.

The Office for National Statistics' *Social Trends* report, an annual snapshot of Britain, said that the figure rose to 42.3 per cent last year.

In 1994, the figure was 32 per cent and in the early 1970s it was less than 10 per cent.

The number of births outside wedlock exceeds 50 per cent in some parts, including Wales. In the North East, it was 54.1 per cent last year.

In London, where a higher proportion of young mothers are Muslims who adhere to more conservative family values, one-third of children were born outside marriage.

The report said Britain now had the fourth highest level of births outside marriage in Europe, after Sweden, Denmark and France.

Much of the rise comes from a sharp increase in people living together. But the number of one-parent families is also increasing.

The figures have alarmed family campaigners, who say the collapse of marriage could have a serious impact on social structures.

They say that most of the statistical evidence suggests that children brought up by married parents do better than those raised by cohabiting couples or lone parents.

Dr Brierley, the executive director of Christian Research, an indep-

By Jonathan Petre, Religion Correspondent

endent organisation that analyses church statistics, said he had tracked birth patterns for his latest publication, *Religious Trends 5*.

'If we get to the stage where more than half of children are born outside marriage, we are fundamentally changing the basis on which society has worked for centuries.

'A whole range of traditional thought about "home", "marriage" and "living together" will have to be re-examined.

'Psychologists say the children from single-parent families do not achieve so much or behave so well as those raised by married families.'

The number of births outside wedlock exceeds 50 per cent in some parts, including Wales

Dr Brierley said his extrapolations show the number of married families will decline from 62 per cent in 2001 to 49 per cent in six years.

In contrast, the proportion of cohabiting couples will rise to about 18 per cent (from 13 per cent in 2001) and one-parent families could represent up to 33 per cent of the population (compared to 25 per cent in 2001).

'There is much more at stake here than statistics,' he said. 'The implications are quite frightening.'

Although much concern has focused on single parents, cohabiting couples also provide less stable backgrounds for children, said the Economic and Social Research Council (ESRC), a government-funded social research body.

John Ermisch, a professor of economics at Essex University, said in a paper for the Council: 'Only 35 per cent of children born into a cohabiting union will live with both parents throughout childhood, compared with 70 per cent born within marriage.'

Campaigners and church leaders have accused politicians of marginalising marriage by undermining its legal and financial privileges and shying away from promoting it above other types of family.

Labour abolished the last tax break for married couples, the Married Couples' Allowance, while its tax credit system is said to favour single-parent families.

Ann Widdecombe, a former Tory Home Office minister, said: 'After the death of the extended family, we are now seeing the death of the nuclear family.

'The long-term consequences are bad for everyone. A well-ordered society is based on the bedrock of marriage, otherwise we will have increasing social disruption.'
21 February 2006

Stepfamilies

Information taken from a ChildLine information sheet

Some facts and figures about the family today

- Recent research indicates that around a half of all divorces will occur within the first 10 years of marriage.
- It is now probable that one in four children will experience their parents' divorce before they reach 16.
- Currently in Britain there are over 2.5 million children in stepfamily life. One million live in their stepfamily; another million visit their stepfamily.

Children are affected by changes in the family. Many children will live in a variety of family environments during their childhood and adolescence.

Stepfamilies

Stepfamilies come together when people marry again or live with a new partner. This may be after the death of one parent, separation or divorce. It can also mean that children from different families end up living together for all or part of the time.

In 2000-2001 over 15,000 children called ChildLine to talk about their family relationships, many of which concerned stepfamilies. A further 1,525 called about parents divorcing or separating.

Some children are very happy, but for others, coping with stepparents, stepbrothers and stepsisters can be a difficult and lonely experience. Settling into a new family situation can always be difficult for the children involved, but this usually resolves itself with time. However, for other children problems can arise in relation to how well they do at school and their general health and well-being. This can result in depression or children feeling stressed and unhappy. What appears to be most important is that children continue to retain a healthy relationship with both their natural parents.

Children have told ChildLine counsellors:

- Michael, 12: 'It's hard getting to know lots of new people all at once.'
- Alison, 15: 'He seems to think he can tell me what to do, but he hasn't got the right. He isn't my real dad.'
- Janine, 13: 'I feel like Mum's a different person.'
- Remi, 13: 'I think that Samuel and his children are more special to her now.'
- Alice, 15: 'It feels wrong when I'm having fun with Dad and his new wife, when I think of Mum by herself.'
- Stef, 13: 'I'm not sure who to go to now, when I want to talk about things.'
- Paula, 10: 'I most want my mum back and for everything to be OK again.'
- Alex, 16: 'Every time I go out with Dad, he quizzes me about Mum and my new stepdad. I feel like a spy.'

Other worries stepchildren may have

Sometimes stepchildren continue to see both their birth parents, but others may lose touch with one of them. There can be pressure to be a 'perfect family', but it takes time to get to know one another.

Just getting used to different ways that each person has can cause problems. Different rules and expectations, kinds of food eaten, when homework is done or what household tasks you would be expected to do are all things that cause stress. Family holidays, Christmas and other religious festivals are all times when each family has its own ways of doing things and it can be hard to adjust to new ways.

Children might have to move house, neighbourhood and school. It can mean losing friends and moving away from loved relatives. Families combining can mean less privacy; for example, sharing a bedroom, or never having somewhere quiet to do homework or just be alone. It can be a difficult time for parents too – they are having to be a parent for a child they hardly know.

How ChildLine can help

It can be hard to find someone with the time to listen when so many changes are happening, and children sometimes feel that they are expected to just get on with it. Although a new family situation won't be the same as before, being part of a stepfamily can be very positive and good for the children involved. It's worth remembering that while things can go wrong, there may also be a means by which to put them right.

Young people may need to go through a grieving process, letting old habits, family ceremonies and ways of doing things go by. They can feel a lot of stress, anger and sadness. Talking can help with all these feelings.

ChildLine takes children's and young people's problems seriously, giving them a chance to talk in confidence about their concerns, however large or small. ChildLine counsellors can also tell them where to go for more information, including local sources of help and advice. This service is free and available 24 hours a day, seven days a week.

Last updated January 2002

- The above information is reprinted with kind permission from ChildLine. Visit www.childline.org.uk for more information. ChildLine and the NSPCC joining together for children.

© NSPCC

Being a stepfamily

Information from ParentLine Plus

Coming together as a stepfamily can be complicated. It might be a time of hope – an opportunity to start again and be a happy and contented family. But a stepfamily is formed when a parent takes on a new partner following a divorce, separation or bereavement. This means children may still be dealing with the absence of a parent and so it may be a long time before a stepfamily feels safe and secure. The best start for a stepfamily is to be aware of some of the challenges ahead. Take things slowly: everyone needs time to adjust.

> *Children may feel that some family members are favoured above others, while the parent and stepparent struggle with feelings of guilt and not knowing how to spread their affections*

Introducing a new partner

To your children, a new partner is a stranger. They'll need time to get to know him or her and to trust them. Introduce them gradually and try not to push your children into giving your new partner affection. Remember that a new partner can never replace a parent but can be an extra support for your children. New partners can help you all to focus on what might work best for the children. As you move together with your relationship, take time to involve your children in changes in living arrangements and hopes for the future.

Finances

In a stepfamily finances can be very complicated. Child support may be going in and out of the household budget at the same time. Try to

Parentline plus

work out with your new partner how you are going to manage the family budget.

Divided loyalties

Within a stepfamily there will be established relationships between biological parents and their children and new relationships forming between children, stepparents and stepsiblings. Children may feel that some family members are favoured above others, while the parent and stepparent struggle with feelings of guilt and not knowing how to spread their affections.

Siblings and stepsiblings may argue initially. However, over time research suggests that stepsiblings can get on and give each other support and friendship.

New ways of doing things

Before coming together as a stepfamily it may be worth working out each other's attitude to raising children. It may be that you need to work out new routines and ways of doing things that are unique to this new family. You will all be learning to share time and space with each other:

- Your child may have to learn how to share you and your ex-partner with others, like stepsisters or stepbrothers.
- Sometimes they may feel that they're not being treated fairly.
- Your child may also have to share their house and possessions with others.

The ex and their relationship with your children

Working out how children stay in contact with your ex-partner can bring additional stress to the stepfamily. Children may react

differently to the new relationship, some may welcome the stepparent, and others will feel hostile to them. Some may even reject the biological parent who is absent from their home for the stepparent.

In most stepfamilies children will be feeling hurt and angry. Try to make arrangements with your ex for your children to see them and with as little conflict between you as possible. Don't get children involved in taking sides. They need to know they are still loved by both their parents. Not to be made to feel guilty that you've split up.

Discipline

How to tackle behaviour that upsets the family is really tricky. It helps if both of you agree on how to handle situations and be consistent in your approach. If you are not the biological parent it is best to invest time in getting to know the children and gaining their trust and respect before attempting to get involved with discipline. Research suggests that how stepdads cope with initial hostility towards them is key to how the relationship develops.

The good stuff

There are very real plus points about stepfamilies. Children and adults can flourish – evidence suggests that living between two households can make a real difference to children's sociability, flexibility, independence and resilience. For parents, sharing the care of their children can provide welcome breaks and a sense of shared responsibility.

Stepfamilies also bring with them new relationships – stepgrandparents and step (or half) brothers and sisters. This means children have more people around who can give them support and guidance.

Parentline Plus tips on stepfamilies

- Give children their own space. When you set up home again with a new partner it is important that all the children have some privacy and a space they can claim as their own.

Evidence suggests that living between two households can make a real difference to children's sociability, flexibility, independence and resilience

---

- Be patient – your children will need time to get to know and trust your new partner and their children.
- Keep a fair approach to all the children – there will be arguments but try not to side with your children rather than your partner's.
- Keep talking – with families joining together it is important to make time to listen to everyone's views and see if there are new ways of doing things that will keep most people happy.
- Allow children to be unhappy sometimes – it may be a new life for you and your new partner but for the children involved it will signal an end. Allow them time to grieve for the old way.
- Involve older children in decisions around sharing two households; take their views into consideration when making future arrangements.

- Listen to your children even if the things they say are negative, it is important that they feel heard. Seek support for yourself if you find it hard to hear the things they say.
- Try to spend time alone with your children to reassure them your love for them has not changed.
- Be prepared – sometimes it may seem that young children have adapted easily to the change in their family but things may come up again when they hit their teens!

Further help

Parentline Plus
- Free, confidential, 24-hour Parentline: 0808 800 2222
- Free textphone for people who are deaf, hard of hearing or have a speech impairment: 0800 783 6783
- Email support: parentsupport@parentlineplus.org.uk
- Website: www.parentlineplus.org.uk

ChildLine
The UK's free, 24-hour helpline for children in danger or distress.
- Helpline: 0800 1111
- General public enquiries: 020 7650 3200
- Website: www.childline.org.uk

National Association of Child Contact Centres
Promotes safe child contact within a national network of child contact centres. A child contact centre is a safe, neutral place where children of separated families can spend time with one or both parents and sometimes other family members. Please call the information line for details of local centres.
- Website: www.naccc.org.uk
- Tel: 0845 4500 280 (Monday – Friday, 9.00 am – 1.00 pm)

National Debtline
A national telephone helpline for people with debt problems. Offers expert advice over the phone and via email. The service is free, confidential and independent.
- Helpline: 0808 808 4000 (Monday – Friday, 9.00 am – 9.00 pm,

Saturday, 9.30 am – 1.00 pm)
- Email advice via the website: advice@nationaldebtline.co.uk
- Website: www.nationaldebtine.co.uk

National Youth Advocacy Service
Provides advocacy services for children and young people up to the age of 25. They provide specialist help in children's rights, children in care, contact issues, education and youth justice. They have a network of advocates throughout the country and their own legal advice team.
- Website: www.nyas.net
- Free helpline for children and young people: 0800 616 101
- Email advice for children and young people: help@nyas.net

Relate
Offers courses on parenting post separation as well as books, advice and local counselling services. Find details of their full range of support and your nearest Relate Centre on their website.
- Tel: 0845 456 1310 (Monday – Friday, 9.30 am – 4.00 pm)
- Website: www.relate.org.uk
- Email: enquiries@relate.org.uk

- The above information is reprinted with kind permission from Parentline Plus. Visit www.parentlineplus.org.uk for more information.

© Parentline Plus

How to be a stepchild

Information from Family Onwards

Today I received an email from a girl, I will call her 'Alison', who told me she was 12 years old and wanted to ask me a question. She went on to say: 'Daddy is going to marry someone else and he is taking me to meet her on Saturday. Please tell me what to do?'

A simple, direct question, but one which set me thinking. It made me wonder how many children there are who are thrust into the complicated arena of stepparents without any idea how to go about it. Or, indeed, what is expected of them.

Has this happened to you? Look in any magazine, and on the Internet, and you will find plenty of advice for parents and stepmothers and stepfathers. There are many organisations, forums for discussion, and conferences planned around the idea of step-parenting. There are plenty of do's and don'ts on offer for parents about how to 'deal' with stepchildren. And yet, you (if you are a child) may find you have been faced – sometimes without warning – with a parent's new boy- or girl-friend. They may even have been introduced, perhaps with a laugh, as your new 'mum' or 'dad". Believe me, this happens more often than you might think.

Perhaps the grown-ups should put themselves in your shoes for a moment. What do we all do when we don't know what is expected of us? What we do, especially when we are uncertain, is to look at the floor, fiddle with our hair, or answer in a monosyllabic way. All ways guaranteed to bring down the wrath of the adults. Perhaps you recognize this?

The difficulty for any child of divorce (and by 'child' I do mean 'adult' children too) is feeling torn between the two people they love most. If on one hand you see mum or dad radiantly happy with a new partner, and on the other a depressed distraught parent, then it is hardly surprising that you view the outsider as the cause of all the family problems. That may not, in fact, be so. But what are you to do? By pleasing one parent, you are likely to feel you are twisting the knife in the other.

> *The difficulty for any child of divorce (and by 'child' I do mean 'adult' children too) is feeling torn between the two people they love most*

A real crisis can occur when there is to be a wedding, just as in the e-mail I received: it had become crunch time for Alison. How can it be that a 12-year-old is so desperate to 'do the right thing' and that I am the only person she can ask? From speaking with many parents over the years, I would guess that 'Dad' is too busy setting up the meeting with his new partner to think just what it means for his daughter. And 'Mum' is the last person to give advice on step-parenting 'etiquette', so Alison is left wondering just what to do, and say, on Saturday.

If you are a parent reading this article, and planning to introduce your children, try to remember that you have had time to know and to grow to love your new partner. Your child will have a very different perspective, and will need time to form a view of his or her own. So, too, will your new partner, who may be scared to death about meeting your child. If you are planning a wedding be extra sensitive to your children's feelings, even in the midst of planning a celebration. They may not feel like celebrating.

So are their any guidelines on 'How to be a stepchild'? If you are old enough to be reading this article you should be aware that you mustn't be rushed into a step-relationship. This may, or may not, happen. Try to get to know your mum or dad's new friend as you would any new person in your life. Then you can decide whether you like them as a person, or not. Accept that by recognizing this new 'someone', you are not necessarily giving the union your blessing. It may be a bitter pill to swallow, but one reason for apprehension and antagonism is often because hopes that your parents will get together again, will be finally dashed. Whether you can allow your parents' new partners to become loving members of your family – well, only time will tell.

So, to all the 'Alisons', remember: nothing you can do can repair the fact that your parents have divorced. If one of them is to remarry, wait and make up your own mind in your own time. So, you don't have to 'do' anything on Saturday. Just be yourself, no more, no less. No one can ask more of you.

And, here is the good news, there is a space for you on this site, so don't feel alone. There is always someone there to listen and to help you over the difficulties of 'being a stepchild.'

■ The above information is reprinted with kind permission from Family Onwards. Visit www.family2000.org.uk for more information.

© Jill Curtis 2005

'Every step-parent fears that they really are a monster'

Stepfamilies are fast becoming the norm – but we still have no idea how to make them work, writes Yvonne Roberts

Annette Mogg has courage in that she is prepared to break the ultimate taboo and talk about living in a stepfamily – honestly. Her son was two when she married Alan, a widower and the father of a boy of eight and two teenage girls. The girls are long gone and the sons are still at home, but eager to leave. The desire for flight, sadly, is common to many stepchildren.

'It was difficult from the word go,' says Mogg, a health visitor from Wimborne in Dorset. 'If I could rewind the video, I would certainly do things differently. I was too strict on my stepchildren because it's easier to be hard if you're not emotionally involved. They would probably agree they were hard on me too.'

We already have at least half a million stepfamilies caring for 2.5 million stepchildren – a figure that excludes the multitude of cohabiting stepfamilies

---

Other people's expectations didn't help. 'People would say, 'Do they call you mum?' The answer was, no they didn't. It would have made me feel quite warm if they had. We paid privately to see a counsellor with one daughter and, if anything, it made it worse. Both girls left at 18 under a bit of a cloud.'

Mogg's son has clashed frequently with his stepfather; recently because he wanted to take the family first- aid box to Glastonbury. 'Alan said what if he wanted something from the box. He humiliated my son in front of his friends. We talked about it later and Alan said that I always take my son's side.'

As well as seeking counselling for one of the girls, the family went to see a counsellor about the depression experienced by Mogg's son. 'That didn't help much. As a health visitor, I run courses for parents of teenagers and my husband attended one of those but that didn't help either . . .

'Even at the age of two, my son reacted as if this was the start of something not quite right. I still feel guilt. I feel I let my son down. I chose the right man for me, but not for him. Our parenting styles are so different, it's driven a huge wedge between us and I feel sad that that has impacted on our children. Perhaps once the boys have left, we'll be able to return to what brought us together 13 years ago.'

Mogg isn't the wicked witch of fairy tales. She is an ordinary person who happened to fall in love with a man who already had children. It happens all the time – yet stepfamilies are barely visible in the landscape of popular culture. We already have

at least half a million stepfamilies caring for 2.5 million stepchildren – a figure that excludes the multitude of cohabiting stepfamilies. At least half of remarriages involving children will also end in divorce and one in four stepfamilies break down in the first year.

It's estimated that if current trends continue, by 2010, divorce, separation and repartnering will the norm. If all this is tough for the adults, it can be diabolical for the children. But apart from the occasional tormented storyline in the soaps,

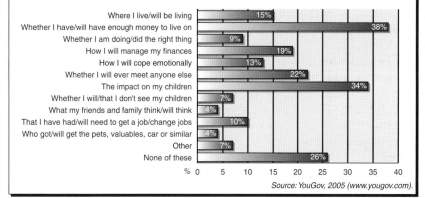

Concerns about divorce

YouGov questioned 3,515 adults aged 18+ (all divorced/separated) throughout Britain online between 31 May and 8 June 2005. Respondents were asked, 'What are your three biggest worries now that you have decided to divorce or separate/ have divorced or separated?' Base: all, unweighted.

	%
Where I live/will be living	15%
Whether I have/will have enough money to live on	38%
Whether I am doing/did the right thing	9%
How I will manage my finances	19%
How I will cope emotionally	13%
Whether I will ever meet anyone else	22%
The impact on my children	34%
Whether I will/that I don't see my children	7%
What my friends and family think/will think	4%
That I have had/will need to get a job/change jobs	10%
Who got/will get the pets, valuables, car or similar	4%
Other	7%
None of these	26%

% 0   5   10   15   20   25   30   35   40

Source: YouGov, 2005 (www.yougov.com).

there's no *Stepfamily Fortunes* or a stepdad stirring in the Oxo cube on the telly. Everybody knows somebody who's a stepchild or step-parent; my father had a stepmother; I've been a stepparent; my partner is a stepfather. In spite of increasing numbers, we appear reluctant to confront why so many of these families are failing – and what can be done to ease the attrition.

We fail, in part, because step-families strain under the weight of trying to masquerade as biological families – instead of acknowledging that we are living with other people's children. In *Stepparenting*, Brenda Maddox's wise and witty book published 30 years ago, she talks of the fallout that comes from uniting 'families with a past'. Maddox was 28 when she married her husband. His wife had committed suicide, leaving a girl of five and a boy of eight. 'The clarity of family life was absent,' she wrote. 'We did not know what we were aiming at.'

Peaceful coexistence, love and laughter might be respectable goals – hard enough at times when there are blood ties that bind (adolescence comes to mind) – but sometimes a dark alchemy takes hold in even the sanest and previously most stable individuals when they become part of 'reconstituted' families.

Children, even the youngest, become adults, and grown-ups react like babies. All parenting consists of an element of anarchy. Everything is going swimmingly then, suddenly, a button is pushed which connects to a parent's childhood experience – and the resulting volcanic reaction can take both child and adult by surprise.

The truth is that 'love will find a way' is a daft piece of blind optimism that has probably mortally wounded more families than we care to acknowledge

---

Add to that the emotions that sometimes (although not always) fester in a non-biological set up – anger, loss, jealousy, resentment, guilt, hatred – then stir that in with two adults who may have diametrically opposed views on what constitutes good behaviour ... and all this happens under the pretence that everything is all right because to confess otherwise is to reveal what every step-parent fears most: that he or she truly is a monster.

Parentline Plus, the national charity offering help and information to families, publishes a report today which analyses recent research including the results of 14,500 calls from stepfamilies to its helpline. The report reveals high levels of depression and anxiety. Other research tells us that a stepfamily in which there is limited yo-yoing between households has a better chance of success. (One teenager I know came for the weekend to discover his stepbrother had been given his room and he was on the sofa.) A new baby can also help to bond the family unit. We know that blue-collar stepdads are much more involved in childcare than white-collar, while lack of cash, space and respite obviously adds to the stress.

Some problems, given time, can be fixed, others can't. A stepchild may want the one thing that a step-parent is unable to provide – unconditional love. Maddox quotes a stepfather who profoundly regretted that he hadn't involved himself more in his stepson's childhood. 'I should have hidden better the lack of love,' he said – raising the question, does a step-parent have a moral responsibility to lie?

Parentline Plus is calling for more sensitivity on the part of professionals – teachers, health visitors, GPs – in their approach to stepfamilies. Mogg was helped by reading leaflets but she also believes that counselling should be far more easily available for stepchildren to access themselves.

The truth is that 'love will find a way' is a daft piece of blind optimism that has probably mortally wounded more families than we care to acknowledge. The abusive stepfather and the hateful stepmother are also a strong part of our mythology. Perhaps it's time we also cultivated fables about stepparents who try their best and, on a modest scale, do achieve miracles. Fables we can believe in, while also conducting a grown-up public debate about the challenges and hurdles – especially for the many children who prematurely leave the family home either of their own volition or because a stepparent has thrown them out.

I know one family in which a never-married man in his 30s moved in with a woman who had a son and a daughter with a severe heart problem and behavioural difficulties. Working as a team, several years on, the family is as solid as a rock.

■ Parentline Plus helpline: 0808 800 2222.
29 June 2005
© *Guardian Newspapers Limited 2006*

Young people talk about divorce and separation

Information from Children's Express

When our mums and dads were growing up, divorce and separation was rare and children whose parents didn't live together were few and far between. But now in the 21st century it's actually not that unusual – in fact you're probably more normal than not.

Recent statistics show that between a half and a third of young people in the UK are likely to experience life in a single-parent family at some stage. That's a lot of young people not only coping with the everyday stresses of growing up, but also the trauma of seeing your parents separate and then having to deal with the inevitable consequences of separation or divorce, like shared contact or not seeing one parent.

It's a lot to deal with when you're young. So how do children and young people do it? And what do they really think about the situation they've found themselves in?

All of the young people we interviewed were not directly involved in the decision-making around where they would live when their parents separated. All of them were now living with only one parent, but most of them had frequent visits with the other parent. Here are their stories.

Ginisha's story

Fourteen-year-old Ginisha from South London was very young when her parents separated. She's been living with her mum ever since:

'It was about two years after I was born and it was because my dad was being abusive towards my mum. He had a drinking problem and they kept getting back together again because my mum thought it would be better if we had a dad in our lives, but he kept on doing it again so they separated. When we came to England they got back together again but after a year,

he got back to doing what he did and so they separated again. They're not together now.'

Ginisha didn't have much say about where she would live when her parents separated for the final time, nor did the courts. But she says she's very happy with the decision that was made:

'I live with my mum and my dad visits when he can. I don't really visit him. I get on better with my mum than I do my dad because he doesn't really treat me appropriately.

When he comes to my house and visits us, we are quite close but sometimes he's in different moods and he acts however he wants towards me and I don't really like that. The tone in his voice also shows me he doesn't really like me much. He says I should have respect for him but he doesn't have respect for me and I think it should work both ways.'

Even though Ginisha says it really hurts her when her father behaves this way on the occasions he does visit her, she says she's happier now because when she was younger and her parents lived together, they fought:

'There wasn't a lot of fights but the ones that did happen, I can remember. It showed me how my dad was towards my mum.'

Unlike some young people who live with one parent but visit the other, Ginisha doesn't have to travel far because her dad lives close by. But she says it can be difficult dividing time between parents:

'Sometimes my mum says things and my dad doesn't agree with it but I know what she says is right, so I just listen to what she says. Sometimes he says bad things about her but I keep it to myself because I don't want her to get hurt. I don't really miss my dad because the way he treats me is not right, but if he gave me a chance to spend more time with him, it might work out.'

Whilst Ginisha says it's hard dividing time between her parents, she clearly would like to spend more time with him and acknowledges that

Access to children after divorce

YouGov questioned 3,515 adults aged 18+ (all divorced/separated) throughout Britain online between 31 May and 8 June 2005. Respondents were asked 'How often do you see your child(ren)?' Base: currently divorcing/separating or divorced/separated less than two years. Males (371) and females (374), unweighted.

	Male	Female
Daily	16%	86%
Several times a week	5%	28%
Weekly	5%	26%
Fortnightly	1%	13%
Monthly	1%	5%
Less often	2%	8%
Never – my partner is preventing me from seeing them	0%	3%
Never – I have been prevented from seeing them by a court order	1%	1%

Source: YouGov, 2005 (www.yougov.com).

its best for a young person to be able to spend time with both parents:

'It's good to have shared contact because if a child lives with only one parent throughout their lives, and they don't see the other parent they may end up hating them because they'll place all of their anger on them.'

And what advice would Ginisha give other young people in a similar situation?

'I'd also say it's important for young people to have a say in the arrangements and for adults to listen carefully to their views because it's really important. Their lives are at stake and if you don't share the arrangements equally, or as your child feels you should, then you'll just end up hurting the child. The child might want to spend time with both parents but if they don't like each other, it will be harder.'

Sabrina's story

Sabrina was 10 years old when her parents separated:

'There were no arguments to speak of,' says Sabrina, who is now 14, as she remembers back. 'There was and still is, nothing around us to upset us,' she adds.

Sabrina acknowledges that it's not been easy but despite the difficulties, she's happy with her situation now:

'Of course it can get a little distressing without both parents in the same house but I don't blame either of them for what has happened. My relationship has got much better with both of them. Seeing my dad is easy as he lives nearby and my

parents are very civilised towards one another.'

Luckily there are now quite a few resources and support services open to young people whose parents have separated or divorced.

One of them is Gingerbread, which is a support organisation for lone-parent families in England and Wales. Gingerbread runs a teens project, which aims to increase confidence in young people who are in lone-parent families, as well as helping them to be more aware of choices in life and encourage school attendance and taking part in youth projects.

'Gingerbread has helped me in so many ways after the upset of my parents separating,' says Sabrina.

'I now know that I'm not the only one in this situation and that itself has helped me so much.'

Scott's story

Scott, 16, is another teenager from a lone-parent family. He lives with his mother in Belfast in Northern Ireland but he still sees his dad.

'It was strange when my parents got divorced. For the first 11 years of my life, I was used to having these people around and then suddenly one of them just disappears. Because you're so young, you never understand what exactly is going on.'

He remembers that his father was always very busy and spent very little time with the family:

'My dad is a chef and has a very stressful job. Because of his job… we sometimes only saw each other a few hours a day. But that isn't to say I wasn't absolutely and utterly devastated when he left.'

Scott's dad is still really busy with work but he enjoys seeing him and says he misses him when he's not around:

'It's difficult because I do get along with my dad better than I get along with my mum. But don't get me wrong, my mum's done an absolutely fantastic job.'

Scott adds that a lot of mothers are more than capable of bringing up children on their own but he thinks it is really important to have two parents:

'The child has that want for this person in their life… As a male you

always look up to your father for that role model in life.'

'When I was younger, I had this insatiable want for that someone in my life to look up to, and even now, I still like the idea of having my own father back.'

Jade's Story

Jade is 13 years old and lives in London. She's never properly spoken to her father and says this has not had much of an affect on her life:

'As my dad left when I was two, it didn't really bother me. How could it? I barely knew him.'

Jade's father has never been in contact with her after failing to turn up to the custody battle in court. But she's not angry and says:

'It made it easier for my mum and I actually. The first time [at court] he came across quite well and the jury felt sorry for him, but the second time, he didn't even show up.'

Jade remains strong about her own situation, but suggests:

'Children need to be listened to. Their parents shouldn't be doing all the decision-making. Just say what you feel and make sure that you're voice is being heard.'

Conclusion

Many young people all over the UK have no other option but to deal with the issues that arise as a result of broken families. More often than not, this means living with one parent and only getting to see the other parent on weekends or sometimes even less frequently. But the young people we spoke to had all learned to deal with things the best they could and most felt happy or at least understood the decisions that had been made by their parents on their behalf.

About the team

This story was produced by Rhona Ezuma 15, Charlotte Lytton, 14 and Modja Hashermyan, 16. It was published by *Magistrate* magazine. *Summer 2005*

■ The above information is re-printed with kind permission from Children's Express. Visit www. childrens-express.org for more information.

© *Children's Express*

Talking to children about divorce

Information from NetDoctor. Reviewed by Joanne M Lee, GP

How do children feel about divorce?

When a couple decide to get a divorce, they usually have some weighty reasons for parting. A divorce will have huge personal and economic effects on a family and it is often the children who are affected the most; they will always experience grief when the parents divorce.

Can you do something that will make the divorce less painful for your children?

Whatever you decide to do to help your children, bear in mind their age and the level of understanding.

A lot of people 'forget' children during the process of divorce

---

A lot of people 'forget' children during the process of divorce. They forget to tell the children about what is about to happen. It is very upsetting for them to be suddenly told that 'Mum and Dad are getting divorced now'.

It is better for the children if they are made aware their parents are talking about a divorce. They can be told for example that 'Mum and Dad have some problems. We don't know how it's all going to end, whether we're going to get a divorce or find another solution. We're working hard to solve the problems and we're getting help.'

Do not involve the children in the discussion; that is way too big a responsibility. They just need to know what is going on. If the children of a couple know at an early stage that their parents may break up, they will not lose trust when the divorce

finally happens. A child also learns that openness is a good thing and that it is OK to talk about problems.

Above all, honesty is a must. When a child asks a question, answer truthfully, even when talking about divorce and what might happen next.

Be aware of what a child's reactions might be and talk about how they feel. A certain amount of self-discipline on the parents' part is required. The divorce is likely to be very difficult to deal with, but sometimes the children must be put first and allowed to express their frustrations and feelings.

How will the divorce affect the children?

They will have two main concerns:
- being separated from one of their parents.
- grief because the original family does not exist anymore.

The children will feel lost. Their own natural place in the family is not the same anymore.

Most children have a 'secret mission' to reunite their parents. If they are asked, they will usually prefer the parents to stay together instead of getting a divorce. This is still the case when the marriage has been very difficult. Children are extremely loyal to their parents. They will often deny and hide their own feelings.

Many children feel guilty when their parents divorce. They think that if they had just behaved better or done better in school, it would not have happened. It is important to explain to a child that they did not cause the divorce. A child needs to know that the divorce is a result of the parents not being able to work things out.

Children often experience a conflict of loyalty. When they are with one parent, they feel guilty

about not being with the other, and vice versa.

It is important, as a parent, to tell a child that it is OK to spend time with the other parent as well. Tell the child that you know they want to be with the ex-partner as well, and that is not a problem.

How will your children react?

Children will always react to a divorce. The question is how and how strongly.

A child who does not show any feelings or reactions needs help to express what is going on inside. Otherwise, they are very likely to suffer depression later.

A pre-school child may show regressive behaviour. This means

that the child may return to an earlier stage of development and, for example, start to wet themselves again. A pre-school child may become confused, irritable or worried.

Children between six and nine are very vulnerable. At this age a child is still not mature enough to understand what is going on, but is old enough to understand that something very unpleasant is taking place. They still depend very much on the parents and will have a hard time talking about their emotions. They may react with anger, or by not concentrating or making progress at school or by having learning difficulties.

Children between 9 and 13 may have started having important relationships with other people besides their parents and family. When the parents divorce, it will often be good for a child to talk to someone outside the family about their problems and feelings. Parents should listen to a 12- or 13-year-old child who says they want to live with one parent rather than the other.

They may react to the divorce with anger, grief or depression.

If a child does not get any better when things start getting back to normal, even when parents talk about what has happened and are very open, counselling can be considered. A counsellor can give advice about how to talk to children. Family therapy can also be considered together with individual therapy for the children.

Trusted good friends can be involved in supporting the children. Group therapy, involving other people in the same situation, can also be a big help.

How can parents make divorce less traumatic for their children?

Talk to the children. Be open; listen to how they feel. They may be angry, frightened or worried. Everybody is entitled to their own feelings; that goes for children as well, though it may hurt a parent to hear how a decision to divorce has affected their children so deeply.

Even if parents and children talked a lot in the beginning, they can still talk about the divorce every once in a while.

Choose a time when both parents and children feel good. Find out if a child has any new questions. Having an open conversation means a lot to the child. If it is not possible to do this oneself, find someone who can, maybe a professional.

Children can express themselves in other ways than with words. Play is very important. Play with the child; let them act out their feelings. Children may need to work off tension through energetic games.

Drawing may help a child. Children often draw things that are important to them. Ask about the drawings; this can be a good way to start your child talking about what's going on inside. Parents should not tell their children off if they don't like what they hear.

Parents should never criticise an ex-partner in front of their child. It can be tempting, but is very unfair. Children know they are part of both parents and they may feel they are as 'bad' as the 'ex' is. When a parent criticises an ex, the parent criticises the child.

Children should not be messengers for parents after a divorce. If a parent needs to tell their ex-spouse something, they should do it themselves. If it is hard for the parents to talk face to face, they should write a letter. It is not fair to use a child as a buffer.

What affects how children will react to a divorce?

Even if parents deal with the problem and talk openly, other things may influence their children's reactions:

- the children's ages at the time of the divorce;
- how smart they are;
- how mature the children are emotionally;
- the children's relationship with both parents;
- how 'bad' the divorce was;
- other people's reactions to the divorce;
- if the children had problems before the divorce;
- whether there are people outside the family who are willing to help.

What if there is a new step-family?

If the children have to deal with a stepmum or stepdad and new brothers and sisters right away, life will of course be even more complicated for them.

Expect difficulties. Children will not like these changes at first. They will need to fight for territory in the new family, both with the other children and with the steparent.

It takes a lot of patience to make this work. A sense of humour helps! It takes time and then more time; it may well be a very long process.
Based on a text by Christel Bech, nurse.

■ The above information is reprinted with kind permission from NetDoctor. For more information, please visit their website at www. netdoctor.co.uk.

© NetDoctor

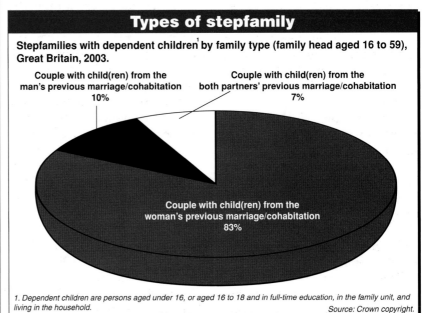

Types of stepfamily

Stepfamilies with dependent children[1] by family type (family head aged 16 to 59), Great Britain, 2003.

Couple with child(ren) from the man's previous marriage/cohabitation
10%

Couple with child(ren) from the both partners' previous marriage/cohabitation
7%

Couple with child(ren) from the woman's previous marriage/cohabitation
83%

1. Dependent children are persons aged under 16, or aged 16 to 18 and in full-time education, in the family unit, and living in the household.

Source: Crown copyright.

Children in one parent families

Information from One Parent Families Scotland

Many commentators have argued that it is less desirable for children to be brought up by one parent than by two parents.

This page summarises recent relevant research which combines the results of many different studies. It also looks at how we can assist children who are adjusting to family change and also those simply living in a stable one-parent family.

Overall effects of separation and divorce on children

Not all children living in one-parent families will have lived with their absent parent. However, for those whose parents were living together there is now a large amount of research showing the effects of family breakdown on children.

The results of a survey based on pooled data from 80,000 adults suggest that parental divorce has an adverse effect on children's lives. Compared with those raised in intact two-parent families, adults who experienced a parental divorce had lower psychological well-being, more behavioural problems, less education, lower job status, a lower standard of living, lower marital satisfaction, a heightened risk of divorce, a heightened risk of being a single parent, and poorer physical health.

The view that children adapt readily to divorce and show no lingering negative consequences is clearly inconsistent with the cumulative research in this area.

However, several qualifications should be noted. Most importantly, the average difference between children from divorced and staying-together families is small.

This suggests that divorce is not as severe a stress for children as other things which can go wrong during childhood. Divorce may represent a severe stress for some children, resulting in a substantial disadvantage and decline in well-being, but for other children divorce may be relatively inconsequential. Some children may show improvement following divorce.

Effects of divorce by gender

For children, research shows that the negative effects of divorce on social adjustment are stronger for boys than for girls. Social adjustment includes measures of popularity, loneliness, and cooperativeness.

In other areas, however, such as academic achievement, conduct or psychological adjustment, no differences between boys and girls are apparent.

The research examining the effects of divorce on adults also shows very little difference between the effects on men and women, with one exception. Although both men and women from divorced families obtain less education than those from continuously intact two-parent families, this difference is larger for women than for men. One possible reason is that non-custodial fathers are less likely to finance the higher education of daughters than of sons.

Effects of separation on different ages of children

Pre-school children
Observation of children during the first year after parental separation showed that pre-school-age children cannot understand the meaning of divorce. Consequently they react to the departure of a parent with a great deal of confusion. Because they do not understand what is happening, many become fearful.

For example, a child may wonder, 'Now that one parent has gone, what is to stop the other parent from leaving also?'

Young children also tend to see themselves at the centre of the world. This leads some children to blame themselves for their parents' divorce. For example, they may think, 'Daddy left because I was bad.' Regression to earlier stages of behaviour is also common among very young children.

Young children
Children of primary school age have greater maturity and can grasp the meaning of divorce more clearly. However, their understanding of what divorce entails may lead them to grieve for the loss of the family as it was, and feelings of sadness and depression are common.

Some children see the divorce as a personal rejection. However because being self-centred decreases with age, many can place the blame elsewhere – usually on a parent.

Adolescents

Adolescents are more affected by their own age group and less dependent on the family than younger children. For this reason, they may be affected less directly by the divorce. However, adolescents may still feel a considerable amount of anger toward one or both parents. In addition, adolescents are concerned about their own relationships.

The divorce of their parents may lead them to question their own ability to maintain a long-term relationship with a partner.

Changes in effects over time

Comparison of early studies of divorce with more recent studies suggests that more recent groups of children are showing less severe effects of divorce than earlier groups. Two explanations are worth considering.

Firstly, as divorce has become more common, attitudes toward divorce have become more accepting, so children probably feel less stigmatised and will find it easier to obtain support from others in similar circumstances.

Secondly, because the legal and social barriers to divorce were stronger in the past, couples who obtained a divorce several decades ago probably had more serious problems and experienced more conflict prior to separation than today.

Why divorce lowers children's well-being

Various reasons can be found for divorce affecting children's well-being. These are detailed below, together with evidence on how the effects can be minimised.

Parental absence

Some studies show that children who experience the death of a parent exhibit problems similar to those of children who 'lose' a parent through divorce. These findings support the view that the absence of a parent for any reason is problematic for children.

Research also shows that children who have another adult (such as a grandparent or other relative) to fill some of the functions of the absent parent have fewer problems than children who have no substitute for the absent parent.

In general, studies show that a close relationship with both parents is associated with positive adjustment after divorce, except in high-conflict divorces, when frequent contact with the non-custodial parent may do more harm than good.

Custodial parent's adjustment and parenting skills

Following divorce, custodial parents often experience depression and anxiety.

Lowered emotional well-being, in turn, is likely to affect their parenting. Children are better off when custodial parents are affectionate, provide adequate supervision, exercise a moderate degree of control, provide explanations for rules, avoid harsh punishment, and are consistent in dispensing punishment.

Research shows that when custodial parents have a good deal of support, their children have fewer difficulties, demonstrating the need for support services and voluntary organisations.

Economic hardship

Divorce typically results in a severe decline in the standard of living for most custodial mothers and their children. Economic hardship increases the risk of psychological and behavioural problems among children and may negatively affect their nutrition and health.

Studies show that children's outcomes – especially measures of academic achievement – are related to the level of household income following divorce. This demonstrates the importance of affordable childcare and effective child support enforcement to reduce economic hardship.

Life stress

In addition to the stresses detailed above, divorce often results in other stressful events for children such as moving house and changing schools. This reinforces the importance for children of improving lone parents' access to permanent housing if they become homeless.

Delinquency

A common assertion is that children brought up in lone-parent families are more likely to become delinquent.

In February 1994 a Family Policy Studies Centre international conference on crime and the family concluded that the main influence on children's behaviour is the parent's ability to supervise their children appropriately, with other factors such as poverty, school failure and lack of self-esteem having less effect. Family structure, whether children are brought up by one parent or two, was of minor significance.

This finding confirmed an earlier study by the Home Office which found that lone-parent families did not have higher delinquency rates than two-parent families.

■ The above information is reprinted with kind permission from One Parent Families Scotland. Visit www.opfs.org.uk for more information.

© One Parent Families Scotland

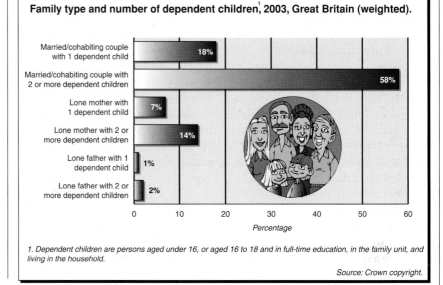

Family types and number of children

Family type and number of dependent children[1], 2003, Great Britain (weighted).

Married/cohabiting couple with 1 dependent child — 18%
Married/cohabiting couple with 2 or more dependent children — 58%
Lone mother with 1 dependent child — 7%
Lone mother with 2 or more dependent children — 14%
Lone father with 1 dependent child — 1%
Lone father with 2 or more dependent children — 2%

Percentage

1. Dependent children are persons aged under 16, or aged 16 to 18 and in full-time education, in the family unit, and living in the household.

Source: Crown copyright.

Lone parent families: action facts

Lone parents and their children now make up an important section of our society. Policies aimed at them will have a significant social effect

How many lone parent families are there?

- Between 1996 and 2004, the number of lone-mother families increased by 12% to 2.3 million.
- In 2004 nine out of 10 lone parents were lone-mothers.

(Statistics taken from ONS. Available online at http://www.statistics.gov. uk/cci/nugget print.asp?ID=1161)

- Between 2003 and 2004, the percentage of lone-parent households (with one child) was 10 times less likely to be on the £500-£600 (a week) income bracket than a two-parent household with one child.

The UK average of lone-parent families is 25.58%

- The highest percentage of income for lone parents was between £100 and £200 per week, whereas for two parent households it was between £800 and £900 per week (both with one child).

(Statistics taken from the Department for Work and Pensions (DWP). Available online at http://www.dwp.gov.uk/asd/ frs/2003 04/tables/pdf/3 5.pdf)

- Labour Force Survey estimates for spring 2005 show the employment rate for lone parents was 56.2%. This is an increase of 5.2% since 2000.

(Statistics taken from ONS. Available on-line at http://www.statistics.gov. uk/cci/nugget print.asp?ID=409)

- The UK average of lone-parent families is 25.58%.
- The highest proportion of lone-parent families is in Lambeth in London, where 48% of families with dependant children

GINGERBREAD
the organisation for lone parent families

are lone-parent families. The lowest proportion of lone-parent families was in the south-east (Wokingham, Chiltern, South Buckinghamshire and Herts) with a percentage of just 13%.

(Statistics taken from ONS. Available online at http://www.statistics.gov. uk/cci/nugget print.asp?ID=1166&po s=3&colrank=2&rank=224)

- The percentage of lone mothers who are economically active has increased from 48% in 1992 to 57% in 2002. With 23% working full time and 28% part time, compared with 31% who stay at home to look after family/home.

(Labour Force Survey, ONS. Available online at: http://www.statistics.gov. uk/statbase/expodata/spreadsheets/ d6253.xls)

- Nearly two million tax credits were overpaid in the tax year 2003-2004. Out of those, 353,000 were to lone parents. The large majority of these overpayments have been made because of serious flaws in the revenues and customs systems. With no limit on the amount of tax credit presently, the amount lone families are left with, while paying back over payments, is well below the Income Support or breadline level.

(One Parent Families. Available online at: http://www.oneparentfamilies.org. uk)

- The Child Support Agency (CSA) has had endless problems since its launch in 1993.
- In 2001, the CSA was owed more than £1 billion in maintenance payments, and had written off

two-thirds as it was uncollectable. In 2003 the new computer and phone system was launched. The system was flawed and technical problems led to only 4% of the 150,000 new claimants receiving a payment.

- In 2004 the unprocessed claims reached 170,00, with 75,000 being lost in the new IT system. The backlog was rising by 30,000 every three months.

(The Guardian, 12/04/05, 'Timeline: the CSA crisis' available online from: http://society.guardian.co.uk/children/ story/0,1074,1457948,00.html)

- The amount of maintenance collected by the CSA has fallen by 2% in real terms.
- The proportion of lone parents receiving a first payment has fallen by one-third.
- The backlog of lone parents waiting for an assessment has increased by 20%.

(The Guardian, 08/09/05, 'CSA is ignoring failures'. Available online from: http://society.guardian.co.uk/ print/0,3858,5280362-110464,00. html)

- More than one million phone calls in 2004-2005 were abandoned as parents give up trying to get through to the CSA.
- The proportion of lone parents receiving a first payment dropped from 72% to 52%.

(The Guardian, 10/09/05, 'Plight of single parents worsens'. Available online from http://society.guardian.co.uk/ print/0,3858,5281767-110464,00. html.)

- Information reprinted with permission from Gingerbread. Visit www.gingerbread.org.uk or call their freephone number on 0800 018 4318 for more information.

© Gingerbread

Mixed blessings?

Raising a multi-racial family. By Claire Benians

What does it mean to be part of a mixed-race family? And what are the thoughts and experiences of mixed raced children?

For the first time in its history, the 2001 Census included the option 'mixed' in its category for ethnicity. This change arose as a result of a growing number of people of mixed race objecting to having to tick the 'other' box on the Census form.

The change also reflects the fact that mixed-race families are among the fastest growing sector of the population in Britain. The overall number of British families of mixed race (a 'family' is defined as a couple with or without dependent children) is small as a proportion of the total 0.6% in the 2001 census. But figures from the Office of National Statistics also published in 2001 show that the number of mixed-race individuals grew by 75 per cent in the 1990s. And of these, more than 50 per cent were aged 11 or less.

What this tells us is that mixed-race families are fast becoming an integral part of Britain's make-up. But what does it mean to be part of a mixed-race family? And what are the thoughts and experiences of parents of mixed-race children? What resources and support groups are there which can help parents?

A mum's story

Laura is white and was brought up in rural Derbyshire. She is married to a British Indian Sikh – they have a nine-month-old daughter, Nina, and live in north-west London. Laura's experience of motherhood with a mixed-race baby has been very positive so far. Laura puts this down to her and her husband's accepting families and living in London.

'Nina recently started nursery. There are so many children of different backgrounds that noone bats an eyelid that my daughter is dark haired and I'm blonde! If we lived where my parents are, in a village in Derbyshire, it might be different – I think London is the best place for us to be.'

Whilst being aware that Nina may have to deal with intolerance in the future, for the moment Laura and her husband are taking things one step at a time. Nina has been to several Sikh celebrations at her local temple as well as traditional weddings in Christian churches. Laura says, 'I think Nina is very lucky to be part of both backgrounds. We are planning to take her to India in the future and show her this aspect of her heritage.

We want Nina to grow up thinking she's nothing unusual.'

Unfortunately, not everyone's experience of life in a mixed-race family is as positive as Laura's. Dealing with prejudice and ignorance can be difficult, particularly when it is your child who is affected. But it is something most mixed-race families have to face up to at some point.

Support

There are a number of organisations out there which aim to help families tackle unacceptable comments and behaviour, whether from members of the public, children's peers or even their own relatives.

Intermix.org.uk is a website where people of mixed race or people in mixed-race families can exchange their thoughts and feelings about their experiences – good and bad – and find out more about the mixed-race experience.

For the first time in its history, the 2001 Census included the option 'mixed' in its category for ethnicity

Intermix advises parents to talk openly at home about race and their family's diversity. Sharron Hall, Editor of Intermix, says: 'It is important to teach your child to be proud of both sides of their heritage. Although there may sometimes be racial tension between races, there are also many good things that come from people of different races getting together and your family is one example.'

When it comes to dealing with racism, the advice is clear: don't let people get away with it. Challenging prejudice – which is so often borne of ignorance – can make people think twice about their views. Sharron Hall

says: 'We would advise parents not to tolerate racially or ethnically biased remarks and to show their children how to deal with such remarks. Of course there are some situations where it is best to say nothing and parents will still have to judge when that is. The personal safety of the family must come first.'

The mixed-race community is one 'which is moving out from the shadows and heading into the light'

People in Harmony (www.pih.org. uk) is a national organisation which aims to support mixed-race families – it 'promotes the positive experience of interracial life in Britain today and challenges the racism, prejudice and ignorance in society.'

Val Hoskins, a trustee of the charity, says: 'A lot of people find talking to others within the mixed-race community extremely useful. Being in a mixed-race family is a positive experience for many, but it does cause confusion to people outside of the experience. People ask questions which aren't necessarily meant to offend, but when they are asked all the time, can seem intrusive.

'We find that members are very happy to be put in touch with others in similar situations. And it's great for children to meet other mixed-race families and to see that people from all sorts of backgrounds together is normal. The questions disappear!'

People in Harmony is also keen to see more consultation with people of mixed race when it comes to policy-making. A recent report from the Department for Education and Skills used the term 'mixed heritage' rather than 'mixed race' – if they had asked people from the community itself they would have found that the term 'mixed race' is actually preferred. Val says: 'The experiences of mixed race pupils should be acknowledged and made more visible within the educational policy, curriculum and the day-to-day practice of schools.'

Despite some of the difficulties, one thing is certain: mixed-race families in Britain will continue to grow. As Yasmin Alibhai-Brown, author of *Mixed Feelings: the Complex Lives of Mixed Race Britons*, says, the mixed-race community is one 'which is moving out from the shadows and heading purposefully into the light, challenging existing ideologies of ethnic and national purity and staking its claims on this nation'. *4 October 2005*

■ The above information is reprinted with kind permission from Families. Visit www.familiesonline. co.uk for more information.
© *Families*

Britain's army of real life 'supergrans'

Information from MINTEL

Latest research from MINTEL* finds that there is more to Britain's grannies than baking, knitting and a round of bridge. The 21st-century granny offers their family invaluable support, providing anything from practical help for the home and financial assistance to regular childcare and even comfort to elderly relatives.

The 21st-century granny offers their family invaluable support

---

Today, more than one-third (34%) of grandmothers look after their grandchildren while the parents are working or simply out and about. This is particularly true of those aged

under 65, with around half (52%) offering some kind of child-care assistance.

'British families are changing rapidly but grandparents are clearly a constant and vital source of support for their children and grandchildren. With many parents now required to work long unsociable hours, grandparents can play an important role in helping with their grandchildren's development while the parents aren't around. Alongside this, grandparents give their own children an element of

freedom so that they can have time for themselves as well as time to work and earn money. For many this independence made possible by Britain's grannies can make all the difference to everyday life,' comments Angela Hughes, Consumer Research Manager at MINTEL.

Looking at this trend in greater detail, MINTEL's research finds that some 16% of all grandmothers take care of their grandchildren while their own son or daughter goes out to work, rising to nearly one in three (29%) of those aged between 55 and 64. Meanwhile, three in 10 (30%) grandmothers act as general babysitters, looking after their grandchildren while their son or daughter goes out.

Today, more than one third (34%) of grandmothers look after their grandchildren while the parents are working or simply out and about

---

'With a growing number of families where both parents work, there is immense competition for childcare whether it is a nanny, childminder, au pair or nursery. As such this care has become extremely expensive, leaving many with no other option but to turn to the grandparents. But there are societal changes working against this trend. The move towards older parenthood and in turn older grandparenthood could mean that grandparents may be less able to help out in the future. Grannies and grandpas today may look younger and seem fitter and more active, but they are actually older than they used to be. Now that women have babies in their thirties and forties, new grandparents are likely to be in their sixties or even in their early seventies and this shift in age may make looking after grandchildren a near impossibility,' explains Angela Hughes.

Today, more than half (54%) of all British grandmothers are aged 65 and over, with just under one in five (19%) aged 55 and under. Just over half of grandmothers are married (55%), and one-third are widowed (33%).

A grandmother's work is never done

Not content with acting as surrogate mothers, today's grannies are taking on a whole host of other family responsibilities. Indeed, it seems that a grandmother's work is never done, with over one in 10 (11%) often helping grown up children (aged 18 and over) and stepchildren with domestic tasks such as cooking, cleaning, DIY and shopping. And it is not just their children who are benefiting from gran's practical help – a further 8% of grandmothers offer similar general household support to an older relative. Meanwhile, one in 20 (5%) look after a relative who does not live with them.

Finally, almost one in five (18%) grandmothers offer regular financial support to their grown-up children (aged over 18), which is particularly surprising bearing in mind that the majority (61%) will be retired pensioners.

'With the onset of the pension crisis, these grannies may well not be enjoying a comfortable retirement. Providing additional monetary assistance to family members could well be placing a significant burden on these women who are already suffering considerable financial pressure,' explains Angela Hughes.

About MINTEL

MINTEL is a worldwide leader of competitive media, product and consumer intelligence. For more than 35 years, MINTEL has provided key insight into leading global trends. With offices in Chicago, London, Belfast and Sydney, MINTEL's innovative product line provides unique data that has a direct impact on client success. For more information on MINTEL, please visit their website at www.mintel.com. *October 2005*

■ The above information is re-printed with kind permission from MINTEL. Visit www.mintel.com for more information.

© MINTEL

'Blended families' and other euphemisms

By Anne Karpf

At noon today, I'll be at a wedding. I'm not the mother of the bride but the stepmother of the groom. This means that I've acquired a delightful new stepdaughter-in-law. As it's a second marriage, the old one (whom I'm still fond of) has now turned into my ex-stepdaughter-in-law – at this rate the world is going to run out of hyphens.

If we were American I suppose you'd call us a blended family, though that makes it sound like we should also be rich, smooth, well-roasted, and possibly Colombian. This euphemism for stepfamilies reeks of *The Brady Bunch*, the 1970s American television series that tried to show step-siblings could come together harmoniously to create a wholesome nuclear family (and that American TV could find something saccharine in just about anything).

> **Step-grandparenting is still such an emerging phenomenon that they haven't had time to create the stereotypes yet**

But practically none of the cliches about stepfamilies have applied to us. My stepchildren were teenagers when I first met their dad. They didn't live with him (and nor did I for the first three years). I wasn't implicated in the break-up of their parents. The guidance usually trotted out on the subject – leave the disciplining to the biological parent, don't try and compete with their real mother – simply wasn't relevant.

Of course this doesn't mean we got through without conflict. There were some pretty rough years in there. Think about mother-teenage daughter hostilities. Then add a 'step' into the pot – the potential for rage increases tenfold.

Death makes it even worse. I know someone whose mother died when she was eight. Within a couple of years her father remarried an altogether saintly woman. Relieved family friends expected the girl to express gratitude. Of course she felt like killing her stepmother, and found many different ways of tormenting her. Children of that age are so awash with fantasies about the power of their feelings that the anger, to a girl whose mother had really gone and died, must have felt very dangerous.

For me and many of the other stepmothers I know, the problems have been aggravated by age difference – I'm roughly halfway in age between my stepchildren and their father, so it's been hard for them and for me to know where to place me. Surrogate parent wasn't an option, but then neither was the friend route. I've worried about them alongside their father, but never as much as I've worried about my own kids. We've had to work out the relationship as we went along, but that goes for all relationships, whatever the idealised images would have us believe.

What makes me part of a social trend is that I'm also a step-grandmother. Grandparents may have been busily throwing off the stereotypes – knitting, rocking chairs, and Madeira cake don't figure any more, but step-grandparenting is still such an emerging phenomenon that they haven't had time to create the stereotypes yet. In America step-grandparents seem exercised about what they should be called – how many grannies can a kid reasonably be expected to have?

My teenager has made the odd attempt to orchestrate my step-grandchildren into calling me 'Granny Annie' (only, of course, because she knows I'd hate it), but thankfully it hasn't caught on. I'd hate it because I don't feel old enough to be a grandmother, though biologically of course I easily am. I had my kids so late that grandparenthood is a stage I only expect to reach in my late 60s or 70s.

So I'm pretty lackadaisical in the role. I'm not bad on birthdays (though I've already forgotten one this year, on account of the house move), quite good on hugs, but I don't feel like their grandparent, and I haven't tried to simulate or manufacture it. They seem OK with that. I've got friends without children of their own, though, who've embraced the relationship with gusto, and the resulting intimacy has been a mutual gift.

In fact what I've enjoyed about being a stepmother and step-grandmother is precisely how little has been expected of me, and how little I've expected. This has made those occasions when my stepkids have spontaneously expressed affection to me (or me to them) particularly touching.

The wedding today, I've just realised, will also supply my step-grandchildren with another set of step-grandparents, along with a couple of step-aunts and a step-cousin. Bring out more hyphens.

15 April 2006

KEY FACTS

- An overwhelming number of today's parents and grandparents believe it is more difficult to raise a family now than it was a generation ago. More than two-thirds (68%) of today's parents say it was easier to bring up children in their parents' day and nearly three-quarters (73%) of grandparents agree with them. (page 1)

- A great number of today's parents (93%) said their parents make good grandparents. (page 1)

- 45% of grandparents said they would like to change something about the way their grandchildren are being brought up. (page 2)

- Grandmothers proved to be far more positive than grandfathers about their children's parenting ability, with 38% of grandmothers rating them a 10 on the parenting scale, compared with just 27% of grandfathers. (page 2)

- Raising a child from birth to 21 costs almost £166,000, according to research. (page 3)

- The rise of the 'adultescent' – grown-up children who still live at home with their parents, is having a major impact on mums' and dads' budgets. A new survey has found that one in three parents are spending as much as £5,000 a year for children over the age of 25. (page 3)

- A new survey reveals that three-quarters of parents would seek support from family, friends or neighbours, compared with less than half who would consult professional or official sources like childminders, health visitors or TV programmes. (page 6)

- Children whose fathers take an active role in their upbringing are more likely to do well at school and avoid getting into trouble with the police. (page 7)

- A study showed that 46 per cent of fathers were reported to play an equal part in parenting in 1958, dropping to 39 per cent in 1970. Only just over one-fifth of men today were satisfied with the number of hours they felt they could spend with their families. (page 9)

- Most dependent children (80 per cent) live with their father, but one in 50 children live only with their father. (page 11)

- Mums work harder than anyone else, putting in at least 100 hours each week in cleaning, childcare, doing the school run and keeping on top of the laundry. This is more than double the 43.6 working week of the average British worker. (page 12)

- Worries about early sexual activity continue to concern parents. 82% of parents raising the issue are worried about young people aged 13 to 15 with 79% about girls. Parents were also concerned about lying and the negative influence of peers. (page 16)

- One in five couples surveyed said that they had come to the decision not to have children at all. More than one-third of those said it was because they were unwilling to compromise their lifestyle, while a further 15 per cent were put off by the cost. (page 18)

- Almost three in ten (27%) parents in 'non-traditional' families worry about paying the bills, compared to just 16% of those in 'traditional' families. (page 20)

- Despite the stereotype of the harassed father 'escaping' to the office, twice as many working mothers (30%) as working fathers (16%) admit that 'going out to work gives them valuable time away from family life'. (page 21)

- Half of all babies will be born to unmarried mothers by 2012 if present trends continue, says new research. (page 22)

- Currently in Britain there are over 2.5 million children in stepfamily life. One million live in their stepfamily; another million visit their stepfamily. (page 23)

- Recent statistics show that between a half and one-third of young people in the UK are likely to experience life in a single-parent family at some stage. (page 29)

- For children, research shows that the negative effects of divorce on social adjustment are stronger for boys than for girls. Social adjustment includes measures of popularity, loneliness, and cooperativeness. (page 33)

- Between 1996 and 2004, the number of lone-mother families increased by 12% to 2.3 million. In 2004 nine out of 10 lone parents were lone mothers. (page 35)

- Mixed-race families are among the fastest growing sector of the population in Britain. (page 36)

- More than one-third (34%) of grandmothers look after their grandchildren while the parents are working or simply out and about. This is particularly true of those aged under 65, with around half (52%) offering some kind of childcare assistance. (page 37)

- More than half (54%) of all British grandmothers are aged 65 and over, with just under one in five (19%) aged 55 and under. Just over half of grandmothers are married (55%), and one-third are widowed (33%). (page 38)

GLOSSARY

'Adultescent'

A term coined to describe grown-up children who still live at home with their parents, a trend which is on the rise due to factors such as rising house prices.

Authoritarian parenting style

This style of parenting is quite strict, with the child being expected to behave and the consequences of misbehaviour being harsh.

Authoritative parenting style

Characterised by parents who allow their children quite a bit of freedom but do have clear standards of behaviour.

Baby boomers

Name given to the generation born during the period of increased birth rates following the second world war, i.e. in the late 1940s and 1950s. Many grandparents of young children in the UK today may belong to this generation.

Cohabiting couple

A man and woman who live together as a couple but are unmarried. Current trends suggest more couples than in previous years are choosing to have children in cohabiting rather than married relationships.

Dependent children

Usually defined as persons aged under 16, or 16 to 18 and in full-time education, who are part of a family unit and living in the household.

Empty nest syndrome

Feelings of sadness and depression experienced when one or more children leave home. More commonly associated with mothers, these feelings can occur in either or both parents.

Family

A domestic group related by blood or marriage living together in a household. A 'traditional' or nuclear family usually refers to one in which a married couple raise their biological children together; however, changing family structures has resulted in so-called 'non-traditional' family groups including stepfamilies, families with adopted or foster children, single-parent families and children being raised by gay or lesbian parents. Research suggests as many as 35% of British parents now live in a 'non-traditional' family group.

Lone/single parent

Someone who is raising a child alone, either due to divorce/separation, widowhood or an absent parent. Research suggests 19% of British parents fall into this group. The majority of these lone parents will be women.

New man

A term coined to describe men who do not subscribe to the traditional view that domestic matters such as child-rearing are primarily a woman's responsibility, and therefore take a more active role in raising their children.

Parental responsibility

Parental responsibility is where an adult is responsible for the care and well-being of their children and can make important decisions about things such as food, clothing and education. Married couples having children together automatically have this right, as do all mothers, but if the parents are unmarried the father only has parental responsibility if certain conditions are met.

Permissive parenting style

Parents in this group allow their children to freely express themselves and do not enforce clear rules on acceptable or otherwise behaviour.

Stepfamily

Stepfamilies come together when people marry again or live with a new partner. This may be after the death of one parent, separation or divorce. It can also mean that children from different families end up living together for all or part of the time. One in four children has parents who get divorced and over half their mothers and fathers will remarry or repartner to form a stepfamily.

INDEX

ADDITIONAL RESOURCES

Other Issues *titles*

If you are interested in researching further the issues raised in *Parenting Issues*, you may want to read the following titles in the **Issues** series as they contain additional relevant articles:

- Vol. 115 *Racial Discrimination* (ISBN 1 86168 348 0)

- Vol. 112 *Women, Men and Equality* (ISBN 1 86168 345 6)

- Vol. 110 *Poverty* (ISBN 1 86168 343 X)

- Vol. 108 *Domestic Violence* (ISBN 1 86168 328 6)

- Vol. 107 *Work Issues* (ISBN 1 86168 327 8)

- Vol. 106 *Trends in Marriage* (ISBN 1 86168 326 X)

- Vol. 75 *Lone-Parent Families* (ISBN 1 86168 264 5)

- Vol. 74 *Money Matters* (ISBN 1 86168 263 8)

- Vol. 22 *Confronting Child Abuse* (ISBN 1 86168 178 X)

For more information about these titles, visit our website at www.independence.co.uk/publicationslist

Useful *organisations*

You may find the websites of the following organisations useful for further research:

- ChildLine: www.childline.org.uk

- Children's Express: www.childrens-express.org

- Families: www.familiesonline.co.uk

- Family Onwards: www.family2000.org

- Gingerbread: www.gingerbread.org.uk

- Home Start: www.home-start.org.uk

- One Parent Families Scotland: www.opfs.org.uk

- Parentline Plus: www.parentlineplus.org.uk

- Raising Kids: www.raisingkids.co.uk

- Right Start: www.rightstartmagazine.co.uk

- SAGA: www.saga.co.uk

- Time Bank: www.realparents.co.uk

ACKNOWLEDGEMENTS

The publisher is grateful for permission to reproduce the following material.

While every care has been taken to trace and acknowledge copyright, the publisher tenders its apology for any accidental infringement or where copyright has proved untraceable. The publisher would be pleased to come to a suitable arrangement in any such case with the rightful owner.

Chapter One: Parenting Issues

Bringing up children, © SAGA, *Today's parents less strict than a generation ago*, © SAGA, *The cost of a child? £166,000 and rising*, © Telegraph Group Ltd, *Parental purse problems*, © Raising Kids, *Parental responsibility*, © Parentline Plus, *Being a parent: the basics*, © Crown copyright is reproduced with the permission of Her Majesty's Stationery Office, *Support for parents*, © Home-Start and Time Bank, *Fathers aren't from Mars*, © iVillage UK, *Styles of parenting*, © RollerCoaster.ie, *The 'new man' myth*, © Telegraph Group Ltd, *Full-time fathers*, © Families, *1 in 3 fathers work 48+ hours a week*, © Crown copyright is reproduced with the permission of Her Majesty's Stationery Office, *100-hour-a-week women*, © Right Start, *Are you a six per center?*, © Raising Kids, *Kid gloves*, © Families, *When parents won't let go*, © TheSite.org, *Parents of teenagers: 'Are we failing as parents?'*, © Parentline Plus, *Family life: the basics*, © Crown copyright is reproduced with the permission of Her Majesty's Stationery Office, *Kids? We can't afford them!*, © Raising Kids, *Friends are the new family*, © TheSite.org.

Chapter Two: The Changing Family

British family life, © MINTEL, *Majority of births will soon be out of wedlock*, © Telegraph Group Ltd, *Step-families*, © NSPCC, *Being a stepfamily*, © Parentline Plus, *How to be a stepchild*, © Jill Curtis 2005, *'Every step-parent fears that they really are a monster'*, © Guardian Newspapers Ltd, *Young people talk about divorce and separation*, © Children's Express, *Talking to children about divorce*, © Net Doctor, *Children in one parent families*, © One Parent Families Scotland, *Lone parent families: action facts*, © Gingerbread, *Mixed blessings?*, © Families, *Britain's real-life army of 'supergrans'*, © MINTEL, *'Blended families' and other euphemisms*, © Guardian Newspapers Ltd.

Photographs and illustrations:

Pages 1, 13, 20, 36: Don Hatcher; pages 2, 15, 28, 38: Angelo Madrid; pages 8, 11, 16, 32: Simon Kneebone; pages 19, 25: Bev Aisbett.

Craig Donnellan
Cambridge
September, 2006